The Economic Analysis of Accounting Profitability

The Economic Analysis
of
Accounting Profitability

Jeremy Edwards
John Kay
Colin Mayer

CLARENDON PRESS · OXFORD
1987

Oxford University Press, Walton Street, Oxford OX2 6DP

Oxford New York Toronto
Delhi Bombay Calcutta Madras Karachi
Petaling Jaya Singapore Hong Kong Tokyo
Nairobi Dar es Salaam Cape Town
Melbourne Auckland
and associated companies in
Beirut Berlin Ibadan Nicosia

Oxford is a trade mark of Oxford University Press

Published in the United States
by Oxford University Press, New York

British Library Cataloguing in Publication Data
Edwards, Jeremy
The economic analysis of accounting
profitability.
1. Accounting
I. Title   II. Kay, J. A.   III. Mayer, Colin
657'.48   HF5635
ISBN 0-19-877241-6
ISBN 0-19-877240-8 Pbk

Library of Congress Cataloging in Publication Data
Edwards, J. S. S. (Jeremy S. S.)
The economic analysis of accounting profitability.
Bibliography: p.
Includes index.
1. Corporations—Accounting. 2. Accounting—Effect
of inflation on. 3. Deferred tax. I. Kay, J. A.
(John Anderson) II. Mayer, C. P. (Colin P.) III. Title.
HF5686.C7E34 1987 657'.95   87-5575
ISBN 0-19-877241-6
ISBN 0-19-877240-8 (pbk.)

Typeset by Cotswold Typesetting Ltd, Gloucester
Printed and bound in Great Britain by
Biddles Ltd, Guildford and King's Lynn

Preface

THIS book has its origins in the Institute for Fiscal Studies (IFS) project on Fiscal Policy in the Corporate Sector. This project made considerable use of company accounting data in analysing the effects of corporate taxation on firm behaviour. In the course of the project careful attention was given to the question of how company accounts could be best applied to economic analyses. This book is the outcome of that assessment.

We have incurred a number of debts to both individuals and organizations while carrying out the work for this book. The Economic and Social Research Council and the Esmee Fairbairn Charitable Trust provided financial support for the IFS project. The Association of Certified Accountants also supported the work reported in Chapter 6 of the book. We are very grateful to these organizations for their help, as we are to Dr Geoffrey Meeks of the Department of Applied Economics of the University of Cambridge, and to Datastream Limited, for providing us with the data on which some of the analysis in the book is based.

Shirley Meadowcroft is owed a particular debt for patiently and efficiently carrying out a great deal of computational work to produce the empirical estimates in Chapters 6 and 7. We have also received a lot of help from a number of other members of the IFS staff for which we are most grateful. An early draft of the entire manuscript was read through and commented upon by Dr Geoffrey Harcourt of the University of Cambridge and Professor Geoffrey Whittington of the University of Bristol, and their suggestions have materially improved the book. We are extremely grateful to these two individuals for their assistance. We must also acknowledge the help that Geoff Whittington's two books on inflation accounting (one written jointly with David Tweedie) gave us in understanding the history and development of the debate on inflation accounting. Needless to say none of the above can be held responsible for any errors in this book.

Finally we would like to thank Indira Dholakia, Christine Molton, Judith Parry, and Nguyet Thu Luu for typing a never-ending series of drafts of the manuscript. Their patience is much appreciated. We are also grateful to Judith Payne for proof-reading the entire manuscript.

Contents

I

Introduction

ACCOUNTING can be defined in general terms as the provision of information relating to economic transactions. Financial accounts are probably the best-known form of accounting: these are the financial statements which are drawn up periodically, primarily for the benefit of the providers of finance for the firm (the shareholders and creditors), reflecting the traditional stewardship role of financial accounting. But the range of users of financial accounts extends well beyond the suppliers of finance to the company, and includes financial analysts, governments, and economists. Examples of the decisions for which the information contained in financial accounts is potentially relevant are the decision by an investor to buy or sell shares in a company; the decision by a company's directors about appropriate dividend distributions; the decision by a creditor to lend to a firm; the decision by regulators as to whether a firm is making excessive profits; and the decision as to whether a particular activity yields a sufficient return to justify its undertaking.

The traditional financial accounts of a company comprise a balance sheet and a profit and loss account. The system of double entry book-keeping is such as to ensure that, in the absence of capital injections or withdrawals by the proprietors, the change in the book value of capital employed is exactly equal to the profit or loss for a period.

It is conventional for accounts to be constructed in historic cost terms. Historic cost accounts value the resources used in the production process at the cost at which they were originally purchased. Likewise the amount that has to be set aside to maintain physical capital intact is calculated in relation to the original purchase cost of the physical assets. Profit is then measured as the surplus accruing during a period over the historic cost of resources employed. The use of historic cost accounts is justified on the grounds of their objectivity (historic costs can be readily ascertained and verified) and the fact that they naturally arise out of the physical transactions of the company. They are frequently described as performing a stewardship role by providing a check on the application of the capital raised by a firm.

This stewardship role is, however, a very limited one, merely recording how funds currently or previously employed are yielding returns. Historic cost accounts provide no indication of the efficiency with which a firm is undertaking its activities since they give no guidance as to the current value of the resources that the firm is employing. Thus a profit in historic cost terms may be the outcome of a change in the value of resources that are being employed in the production process since the date at which they were acquired. Alternatively the firm may indeed be earning a profit on and above the amount that could be raised from employing the assets in their next best alternative. Historic cost accounts are not able to distinguish between these two possible explanations. For this purpose the current value of the company's assets is required.

There are three current valuation bases for assets which represent the value of currently available opportunities: replacement cost, net realizable value, and present discounted value of future net cash flows. All three have their supporters (see Whittington (1983) ch. 5). Following Hicks' classic analysis of income concepts (Hicks (1946)) there is now virtually universal acceptance in the academic literature of the view that income measures should be based on the present value of the earning power of an individual or a firm. Hicks defined income as 'the maximum value which [a man] can consume during a week, and still expect to be as well off at the end of the week as he was at the beginning' (Hicks (1946)). The analogous definition of a company's profit is the maximum value which a company can distribute during a period, and still expect to be as well off at the end of the period as it was at the beginning. If 'as well off' in the above definition is interpreted to mean owning assets with the same present value, then the profit figure which results from accounts using present value as the valuation base corresponds to Hicksian income for the company (assuming that expectations were fully realized during the period in question). Hicksian or economic profit for a period under this approach is given by the present value of future net cash flows at the end of the period less the present value of future net cash flows at the beginning of the period plus the net cash flow arising within the period after adjusting for the introduction of new capital during the period.

There are two major problems that are encountered in trying to apply the Hicksian definition of profit to an accounting concept. First, the accountant is being asked to provide an estimate of the present value of future cash flows. This prediction is clearly going to be highly subjective and open to contentious disagreement. It certainly does not enjoy the advantage possessed by historic cost accounts of being readily verifiable. Furthermore it could be argued that accountants' estimates of present value are likely to be inferior to those generated on the stock market. According to one body of theory, the stock market impounds most, if not all, relevant information about the firm's future prospects (see Fama (1970), Grossman and Stiglitz (1980)).

Secondly the profit concept described above as the difference between opening and closing present values plus net cash flows during the intervening period is an *ex post* one. It only provides a guide to the profit distribution of a firm if it is expected that this profit will be maintained in the future. In other words what happened *ex post* may be affected by unanticipated events, luck or misfortune, which will not be indicative of likely future performance. If expectations were not fulfilled during the period then it would be inappropriate to base distribution decisions (in the case of a firm) or consumption decisions (in the case of an individual) on actual out-turns. Instead, unanticipated components will have to be excluded from the backward-looking income and profit measures if they are to be relevant indicators of sustainable earnings.

The measurement of Hicksian or economic profit of a company thus presents severe practical difficulties for accountants. So much so that some have argued that accountants should not try to calculate economic profit (Treynor (1972)) and that accountants should not try to estimate present value but should concentrate on supplying relevant information to users of accounts who will form their own estimates of present value (Bromwich (1977), Peasnell (1977)). Indeed it is clear that it is this latter role of accounting information which is its major one: in general investors, regulators, economists, and other users of financial accounts are attempting to assess the performance of firms, either prospectively or retrospectively, rather than looking to the accounts for an estimate of the maximum sustainable distribution that the company can make. This information is then impounded in the company's stock market value, and if the firm's stock market value is taken as the best available estimate of its present value, then economic profit for a period can be straightforwardly estimated as present value at the beginning of the period multiplied by the real discount rate.[1]

Thus the Hicksian definition of profit can be directly ascertained from market valuations and the real discount rate. Accounts would appear to serve no independent function except in so far as they contributed to the determination of appropriate stock market valuations.

Against this background, it is perhaps curious to note that there is a substantial economics literature that has used the profit estimate from company accounts directly. Many examples of the use of accounting information can be given. Rates of profit have been calculated at an aggregate level, either for manufacturing industry as a whole or for particular industrial sectors, using national accounts data for individual countries. Underlying such calculations is the view that changes in these aggregate accounting rates of profit are indicative of changes in the incentive to invest in particular economies. Studies of this type include the regular estimates of company profitability in the UK produced by the Bank of England (in the June issue of the Bank of England Quarterly Bulletin) following the original work by Flemming *et al.* (1976) (see also Williams (1981)); those by Feldstein and Summers (1977) and Holland and Myers (1979) in the USA, and the comparative study of profitability in seven countries by Hill (1979).

Accounting rates of profit are also widely used in industrial economics. There are a number of well-known hypotheses concerning the relationship of the profits earned by a firm or in an industry as a whole to the number and size of firms in an industry (the concentration of the industry) and the degree of potential competition from firms outside the industry, which in turn is affected by the presence of economies of scale, sunk costs, product differentiation, brand loyalty, and so on (i.e. barriers to entry). These hypotheses have been subjected to extensive empirical testing, and in many of the empirical studies rates of profit obtained from company accounts have been used to measure firm or industry profitability (see Hay and Morris (1979) chapter 7 for a review of the relevant empirical work).

A related area in which accounting rates of profit are used is in competition policy. In the UK, investigations into the competitive structure of an industry are undertaken by the Monopolies and Mergers Commission. According to Fairburn (1985), the typical use of profitability figures by the Commission comes at the stage after the market power of the firm under investigation has already been established to some degree by other forms of analysis (and indeed further analysis may follow, to check that high profits are the result of the company's market position). The accounting rates of profit are not used to assess the degree of market power but rather to derive conclusions as to whether a situation is against the public interest. Generally this is done by comparing the company's accounting rate of profit with the average accounting profitability of manufacturing industry as a whole, or perhaps the average for the particular industry in which the company operates. The Commission tends to make an adverse finding only if the company's accounting rate of profit greatly exceeds the average—i.e. is three or four times as high, or more. It is clear therefore that accounting rates of profit play a significant role in UK competition policy. Accounting rates of profit are also important in anti-trust policy in the USA,[2] where they are used as a means of regulating potentially monopolistic utilities in the private sector: a minimum rate of profit on capital is specified for the utility.

Accounting rates of profit are thus widely used, by economists and others, to assess the performance of activities such as firms, industries and entire sectors. The theoretical basis for this use of accounting rates of profit is, however, far from clear. The activities whose performance is being assessed all have the general characteristics of investments, in that they involve forgoing potential consumption in the prospect of generating future returns. Therefore the natural way in which to attempt to give a firm grounding to the use of accounting rates of profit in the assessment of the performance of these activities is in terms of the theory of optimal investment decisions. But this theory suggests that in general the way to appraise investments is by discounting the net cash flows generated by an investment using as discount rate a measure of the opportunity cost of the funds tied up in the project, and comparing the resulting figure with the initial cost of the investment—the net present value approach. In some cases it is possible to make optimal investment decisions by calculating the discount rate at which an investment has a zero net present value—which is known as the internal rate of return—and comparing it with a measure of the opportunity cost of funds. If the accounting rate of profit of an activity corresponded to its internal rate of return, then the use of accounting rates of profit as summary indicators of performance, to be compared with the opportunity cost of capital, could be justified.[3] But unfortunately matters are not that simple.

First, investment appraisal using the internal rate of return will not always yield correct results, so that this method of assessing investments is inferior to the net present value one. In particular, as we discuss in Chapter 2, the internal rate of return method may not yield a single solution, and interpretation of multiple solutions is difficult. Second, even putting aside the drawbacks of the internal rate of return as a method of investment appraisal, the accounting rate of profit, which is measured at a point of time as the ratio of accounting profit to book value of capital employed, is a different concept from the internal rate of return, which is the discount rate that makes the present value of the flow of receipts and expenditures attributable to an investment over its lifetime zero. There have been a number of analyses of the relationship between these two concepts, the conclusions of which make depressing reading: accounting rates of profit do not in general coincide, even on average, with the corresponding internal rates of return. The following quotation from Turvey (1971) is probably representative of currently prevailing opinion: 'the accounting rate of return on total assets . . . means little. In particular it does not approximate the average of the d.c.f. [i.e. internal] rates of return on past investments and so does not indicate whether these past investments were, on average, reasonably successful'.

These deficiencies of accounting rates of profit as summary indicators of the performance of investments are quite widely appreciated, at least among economists. Thus both Feldstein and Summers, and Hill in the studies mentioned above state that their measures of profit rates are exact measures of the internal rates of return on investments only under particular assumptions about depreciation and in general can only be taken as approximations to internal rates of return. In the industrial economics literature, however, other measures of profitability have been used in order to avoid the problems with accounting rates of profit—examples are the ratio of profits to sales revenue, which under constant returns to scale is equivalent to Lerner's index of monopoly power (price minus marginal cost divided by price), and Tobin's q (the ratio of the firm's market value to its replacement cost), as recently used by Lindenberg and Ross (1981), Salinger (1984), and Smirlock *et al.* (1984).

Nevertheless, accounting rates of profit continue to be widely used to assess performance, both by economists and others. This can in large part be explained by the ready availability of accounting profitability data, and the fact that a rate of profit or rate of return concept has considerable intuitive appeal as a potential method of assessing the performance of investment activities.

Our objective in this book is to try and justify the use of accounting rates of profit in the assessment of the performance of activities, developing arguments put forward in Kay (1976) and Kay and Mayer (1986). We contend that the

Hicksian definition of income is not in fact the one that is most relevant to establishing the profit of a firm or industry. Income and profits are different concepts, and while that distribution which leaves future earning power unchanged is of some interest, it is not the one that is most relevant to answering the questions in which investors, financial analysts, regulators, and economists are most interested. Instead what is required is a measure that tells us the benefits from undertaking one activity rather than another. What is the gain to be derived from additional investments in an activity as against investments elsewhere? To what extent has a firm operating in a particular industry derived benefits from that industry as against another?

In this book we argue that the internal rate of return is the correct approach to answering these types of questions only under certain circumstances. In particular, for a project whose net earning stream over its entire life is known, the internal rate of return should be compared with the cost of capital along the lines mentioned above. Furthermore, as demonstrated in Chapter 2, the internal rate of return of such a complete set of cash flows can be derived precisely from any accounting rate of profit concept. Thus accounting numbers are relevant in this case, but only to the extent that they can be used to replicate cash flows and thereby generate internal rates of return.

While of some value, this result is not of very profound interest. More pertinent is the question of what is the appropriate measure of profit for any activity whose performance can only be monitored over a limited segment of its life. It is the central purpose of the book to demonstrate that there is a set of accounting rules which are appropriate for answering questions about investment or disinvestment, or entry into or exit from an industry over a finite segment of a firm or industry's life. Furthermore this set of accounting rules has received a wide measure of support from the accounting profession. Many of the conventions that are currently employed approximate these rules and what this book does, in particular in Chapter 4, is to provide a strong theoretical justification for a set of rules that many regard as intuitively appealing.

The reason why the conclusions of this book are so very much more positive about the role of accounting information in economic analysis than previous studies is that, in our view, previous studies have been applying the wrong standards against which to judge accounts. The appropriate criterion is *not* whether accounting rates of profit equal internal rates of return—nor is it whether accounting profit equals Hicksian profit. The latter is relevant to establishing the level of distribution that can be maintained i.e. permanent income streams. It is not relevant to answering questions about expansion or contraction of a firm or industry or about the relationship between returns being earned in different sectors. That is what will concern us in this book and it is our view that it is this set of issues that has been at the heart of many previous economic studies which have used accounting profitability data. The internal rate of return concept is designed to address these questions but it has little to say about how evaluation over a finite segment of a firm's life should be made.

Our concern then in this book is to establish the set of accounting rules under which the answers to economically interesting questions can be derived. As we demonstrate in Chapter 4, these rules are really most straightforward and could in practice be implemented without undue measurement difficulties being encountered. If these rules were implemented then this book suggests that accounts would be of real practical value to a wide body of individuals: investors, regulators, managers, and economists. Furthermore, once these rules are appreciated, then the resolution of some major controversies that have bedevilled the accounting profession for so long would be immediately apparent. Neither inflation nor deferred taxation present particular difficulties for implementing the set of rules that we and many others have advocated. Inflation corrections are readily and conveniently computed and the extent to which provision for deferred taxation should be made follows immediately.

The plan of the book is as follows: in Chapter 2 we set out the essentials of the standard theory of optimal investment decisions, comparing the net present value and internal rate of return approaches, and then discuss the relationship between the accounting rate of profit and the internal rate of return in some detail. The various analyses of this relationship which have led to the view represented by the above quotation from Turvey are surveyed briefly. However, it is then shown that a number of general results relating the accounting rate of profit to the internal rate of return are available if the accounting profitability data cover the entire lifetime of the investment: in particular in this case it is always possible to deduce the internal rate of return from accounting profitability data so long as the accounts are fully articulated.

In Chapter 3 however, we consider the point that in many, perhaps most, cases the available accounting data will cover only a segment of the lifetime of an investment, and when this segment is short relative to the complete life of the investment, accounting data provide little useful information about the investment's internal rate of return. But in such cases it is not clear that calculation of an investment's internal rate of return is the appropriate way to assess its performance over a segment of its lifetime, because the internal rate of return is defined as a single figure irrespective of the duration of the investment. In Chapter 3 we define an alternative rate of return concept for summarizing the performance of an activity over a finite segment of its life—the accounting rate of return. As its name suggests this is based on accounting data, and the basis on which book value of capital employed is determined becomes crucial for giving any economic interpretation to this rate of return concept. We argue in Chapter 3 that assets should be valued on the basis of the value-to-the-owner rules, and we consider some of the practical problems involved in implementing these valuation rules.

In Chapter 4 we show that the accounting rate of return computed over a segment of an activity's lifetime, using value-to-the-owner rules for book value of capital employed, can provide economically relevant information, in the sense that it can be compared meaningfully with a measure of the opportunity cost of capital over the segment. Thus investors, financial analysts, regulators, and economists can, in certain circumstances, use accounting profitability data in order to give relevant answers to a range of different questions.

Chapter 5 considers the implications of the analysis in Chapters 3 and 4 for the debate on inflation accounting. On the basis of that analysis we argue in favour of the approach to inflation accounting known as Real Terms accounting, in which a current valuation base for capital employed (the value-to-the-owner rule) is combined with a general index adjustment for the effects of inflation. We argue that this form of inflation accounting, which has a distinguished intellectual history, is superior to the two better-known methods of inflation accounting, Constant Purchasing Power and Current Cost accounting.

In Chapter 6 we illustrate the quantitative significance of the differences between Real Terms, Constant Purchasing Power, Current Cost accounting, and Historic Cost accounting profitability measures. We do this in two ways: first by examining the profitability figures that the different approaches produce under various hypothetical situations and second by estimating profitability figures on the different bases for a sample of British companies over the period 1966–81.

Chapter 7 considers the implications of the analysis in Chapters 3 and 4 for the issues involved in accounting for deferred taxation. The various ways in which deferred tax has been accounted for are described, and it is shown that, in the case where accounting data over the complete lifetime of an investment are available, any method of accounting for deferred taxation which is fully articulated and takes deferred tax balances from an initial value of zero to a corresponding final value of zero will permit the post-tax internal rate of return to be calculated from post-tax accounting profitability data. This result is of limited value however: interest is more likely to be focused on performance over a segment of an activity's lifetime. We show that the analysis of Chapter 4 can be straightforwardly adapted to cover the case where companies are subject to taxation. If the accounting rate of return over a segment of an activity's life calculated from post-tax accounting profitability data and initial and final valuations of capital employed is to be relevant for economic analysis then the deferred tax balance in any period must be such as to translate the book value of capital employed from value to the owner before tax to value to the owner after tax, and all changes in the deferred tax balance from period to period must flow through the profit and loss account via the transfer to or from the deferred tax account. We then illustrate how these principles for deferred tax accounting can be applied by calculating a post-tax accounting profitability measure for a sample of UK companies.

Finally, Chapter 8 draws together the main themes of the book.

There are some general features of the argument in the book which it is useful to set out at the start. Our aim is to argue that a rate of return which is relevant for economic analysis can be defined over a segment of an activity's lifetime and, under certain conditions, this rate of return can be measured using accounting profitability information. The justification for the claim that this rate of return is relevant for economic analysis comes from the fact that a comparison of this rate of return with a measure of the opportunity cost of capital allows relationships between the present value, replacement cost, and net realizable value of the activity at the start of the segment to be inferred. Thus the aim of this part of our argument is to give the intuitively appealing use of a rate of return measure to assess the performance of an activity (by comparing it with the opportunity cost of capital) a solid grounding in terms of the net present value method of investment appraisal—the method supported by the theory of optimal investment decisions. A critical assumption in deriving the net present value rule for investment appraisal is that capital markets should be perfect and complete: without this assumption it is very difficult to have any general theory of optimal investment decisions. The extent to which this assumption is not satisfied in practice is difficult to judge: our analysis, which argues for particular measures of accounting profit and book value of capital to be adopted so that the resulting accounting rate of profit can be justified as a summary performance indicator in terms of the theory of optimal investment decisions, rests on the view that departures from the ideal of complete and perfect capital markets in reality are not that significant. Such an assumption is, however, implicit in most other uses of accounting data.

Our analysis, arguing as it does for a particular way of measuring accounting profit and book value of capital, may seem to be in conflict with a view that has developed in the academic accounting literature according to which emphasis on a single profit measure, or a single summary measure of economic performance, is misplaced. This approach argues that in a world of uncertainty, with imperfect and incomplete markets, it is not possible to define a single unambiguous measure of the 'true' value of the firm's assets or its 'true' profit for the period, and hence accounts should report a variety of measures of these concepts, which can be used by different users for different purposes, and are all potentially useful sources of information for the estimation of the firm's future uncertain cash flows. This view (an example of which is Beaver (1981)) is largely concerned to argue against accounts trying to report a single measure of economic profit, because it regards the purpose of accounts to be the provision of information which is useful for the estimation of economic profit. It will be clear from the earlier discussion that there is in fact no conflict between this approach and our argument: we do not regard the reporting of economic profit to be a suitable function of accounts, and agree that accounts should rather provide information which will be useful for estimates of economic profit and present value. But, as we have argued, accounting information is widely used to assess performance, and this is commonly done by means of the accounting rate of profit. It must be recognized that this function of accounts is distinct from that of general provision of information relevant to the assessment of future net cash flows, and our purpose is to argue that there is a correct way to measure accounting profit and book value of capital if the objective is to calculate an accounting rate of profit which will be compared with the opportunity cost of capital in order to assess performance. Our concentration on the single correct way of measuring profit and capital for this purpose does not mean that we exclude other measures of profit and capital for other purposes. We are broadly sympathetic to the view that accounts should report a wide range of potentially relevant information.

One other general point which should be made at the outset is that accounting profitability data can, by their very nature, only provide information about the *financial* rather than *social* appraisal of investments. The latter differs from the former, of course, by taking account of certain social costs or benefits which do not appear as private costs or benefits in the financial accounts. It is well known that the private profitability of an action is not always the same as its social desirability, and this should be borne in mind in what follows. Statements of the form that an accounting rate of return less than the cost of capital indicates that exit from an industry is appropriate are to be interpreted as referring to the appraisal of this action on a financial rather than a social basis.

Notes

1. This can be seen as follows. Let D_t^e denote the distribution in period t expected at the start of period 1, ρ the one-period discount rate (assumed constant), PV_0 the present value at the beginning of period 1 (end of period 0) and PV_1^e the present value at the end of period 1 (beginning of period 2) which is expected at the start of period 1. By definition

$$PV_0 = \sum_{t=1}^{\infty} \frac{D_t^e}{(1+\rho)^t} = \frac{D_1^e}{1+\rho} + \frac{PV_1^e}{1+\rho}. \tag{1}$$

The company's Hicksian or economic profit in period 1 is the maximum distribution it can make during period 1 and still expect to have the same present value at the end of the period as it does at the beginning. Using equation (1) we find that

$$PV_1^e - PV_0 = \rho PV_0 - D_1^e$$

so that the maximum distribution it can plan to make in period 1 while expecting to have an unchanged present value at the end of the period is ρPV_0.

Note that, in order to take account of Scott's point that changes in value due to expected changes in (one-period) discount rates must be excluded in order to estimate the maximum sustainable distribution in this way (Scott (1976)), the discount rate which should be used in practice to estimate economic profit from stock market values should be based on long-term real interest rates.

2. It was the recent US versus IBM anti-trust case which inspired the particularly virulent denunciation of the relevance of accounting profitability measures as indicators of the economic rate of return by Fisher and McGowan (1983) which is discussed in Chapter 2.

3. In terms of the notation in note 1, this can be seen as follows. If accounting profit in period 1 equals economic profit it is ρPV_0 and if book value of capital at the start of the period is PV_0, the accounting rate of profit in period 1, defined as accounting profit divided by book value of capital employed at the start of the period, is ρ.

2

The Assessment of Complete Activities using Accounting Profitability Data

THE purpose of calculating a rate of profit on capital is usually to assess the performance of the investment involved in using a sum of capital in a particular way. The assessment may be *ex ante*, in which case its purpose is to decide whether a particular investment project should be undertaken, or *ex post*, in which case the object is to determine how well an investment which has already been made has performed. The investment in question may be a single project, such as the building of a new factory or the purchase of a new lorry, or it may be the operation of an entire firm or industry. Both single projects and the operation of an entire firm or industry have the characteristics of investment in that they involve a sacrifice in one period and gains (which may turn out to be negative) in subsequent periods. The initial sacrifice in the case of a single project is obvious: in the case of an existing firm the sacrifice is the value (appropriately defined) of the firm's assets at the start of the interval over which its performance is assessed. We shall use the term 'activity' throughout the book to refer both to single projects and to the operation of firms or industries. The assessment of the activity may be from the point of view of an individual firm or it may be from the point of view of the efficient use of an economy's overall resources. In all these cases the aim of calculating the rate of profit on capital employed is to compare it with a measure of the opportunity cost of the capital employed and, on the basis of this comparison, assess the desirability of the activity. Thus one would like to be able to say that if the expected rate of profit on a new factory exceeded the opportunity cost of capital then the factory should be built, or that if the rate of profit earned in a particular industry exceeded the opportunity cost of capital then that industry should expand.

The extensive literature on the theory of optimal investment decisions[1] has, however, shown that great care must be exercised in assessing investments by comparing their rates of profit with a measure of the opportunity cost of capital. Indeed it is now generally accepted that if capital markets are perfect, a firm acting in its shareholders' interests should assess investments on the basis of their net present value rather than by any rate of profit measure. Section 2.1 of this chapter illustrates the use of net present value and discusses the difficulties involved in appraising investments on the basis of the alternative internal rate of return approach.

The conceptual problems encountered in Section 2.1 arise even before any questions of measurement are addressed. A widely used source of information on performance is that available from company accounts. In particular statements about company profits would appear to provide data relevant to investment analysis. But, as Section 2.2 describes, the purposes for which accounts are constructed are by no means restricted to investment analysis and the conventions that are followed in devising accounts are not, as a consequence, the ones that are most suitable for investment appraisal. Indeed it has been suggested by several authors that accounting statements of rates of profit provide no guidance whatsoever regarding the underlying economic performance. These criticisms of accounts have received widespread attention, and Section 2.3 thus devotes some time to a careful presentation of these arguments.

There is one set of circumstances in which the criticisms of Section 2.3 are unduly pessimistic. Where complete data over the entire lifetime of a project are available, then precisely relevant economic information can be obtained from accounting profitability figures. Indeed there are a number of important results that can be derived for self-contained data on an activity, and Section 2.4 is devoted to a description of these results. Section 2.5 thus concludes by noting that although caution is needed in the use of accounting profitability data, it is not the case that accounting information can be rejected out of hand as irrelevant.

2.1 Investment appraisal

The present value of an investment is given by discounting all the net cash flows it generates over its life at a rate given by the appropriate opportunity cost of capital. The opportunity cost of capital should reflect both the time value of money and the risk involved in the investment. Subtracting the initial cost of the investment from its present value gives net present value. If capital markets are perfect then firms acting in their shareholders' interests should undertake investments with net present values greater than zero, and should reject investment projects with net present values less than zero.

The discount rate used in the net present value calculation represents the opportunity cost of investing in the activity rather than on the capital market. The opportunity cost of capital is the highest return that shareholders could have earned elsewhere on the equity capital that is invested in the firm. Although the basic idea of the opportunity cost of capital is straightforward, measuring it in practice is less clear-cut, as it is necessary to allow for risk (so that the assets which shareholders could invest in directly must be ones with risks equivalent to the activity under consideration) as well as the influence of taxes and the fact that investment funds come from several different sources. There is an extensive literature on the measurement of the cost of capital to a firm which we shall simply note: Brealey and Myers (1981, chs. 16–19) provide an excellent introduction to the issues involved. We shall simply assume that the appropriate cost of capital is known.[2]

It is useful to consider a simple example of the net present value of an investment project. Consider an investment project involving the purchase of an asset for £100 at the end of period 0 which generates positive cash flows at the end of each of the next four periods. It is assumed that there is perfect certainty, so that no distinction need be made between the *ex ante* and *ex post* assessment of a project. The net cash flows associated with the project are shown in Table 2.1, together with its net present value for various different discount rates. The general expression for net present value can be written as

$$\text{NPV} = \sum_{i=1}^{n} \frac{C_i}{\prod_{s=1}^{i} (1+\rho_s)} + C_0 \tag{2.1}$$

where C_i denotes net cash flow in period i, ρ_s denotes the one-period discount rate (or cost of capital) between periods $(s-1)$ and s, and the project lasts from period 0 to period n. In the case where these one-period discount rates are all constant over the life of the investment, equation 2.1 simplifies to

$$\text{NPV} = \sum_{i=1}^{n} \frac{C_i}{(1+\rho)^i} + C_0 \tag{2.2}$$

where the time-period subscript on ρ has been dropped as it is now constant. If the one-period discount rate (or cost of capital) is constant at 10 per cent, the net present value of the investment shown in Table 2.1 is 26.87, so that it should be undertaken. If the one-period discount rate is constant at 20 per cent, the project has a zero net present value, and so is just acceptable, while if

Table 2.1. Net cash flows and net present value (NPV) of a project

	Period				
	0	1	2	3	4
Net cash flow	−100	12	43.2	69.12	41.47
NPV (constant 10 per cent discount rate)			26.87		
NPV (constant 20 per cent discount rate)			0.00		
NPV (constant 30 per cent discount rate)			−19.23		
NPV (varying discount rate)[a]			11.07		

[a] See text for details.

the one-period discount rate is constant at 30 per cent, the project's net present value is -19.23 and so it should not be undertaken. The case of a constant one-period discount rate is special, and in general the one-period discount rate is likely to vary over time. There is no difficulty in using the net present value rule in such circumstances: if the one-period discount rate was 10 per cent between periods 0 and 1, 20 per cent between periods 1 and 2 and periods 2 and 3, and 10 per cent between periods 3 and 4, the net present value of the project shown in Table 2.1 would be 11.07, so that it should be undertaken.

If the consensus of the theoretical literature on optimal investment decisions is that the net present value rule is the appropriate one to use for investment appraisal in most cases,[3] does this mean that investments cannot be assessed by comparing their rate of profit with the cost of capital? The answer is no: in certain circumstances optimal investment decisions can also be made by accepting activities whose rate of profit exceeds the cost of capital. It is, however, necessary to define the rate of profit carefully if optimal investment decisions are to be made in this way, and to emphasize this point the correctly defined rate of profit is usually referred to as the internal rate of return of the activity.

The internal rate of return (henceforth IRR) is that constant one-period discount rate which makes the net present value of an investment zero. Formally the IRR is defined as r such that

$$\sum_{i=1}^{n} \frac{C_i}{(1+r)^i} + C_0 = 0. \tag{2.3}$$

In the example of Table 2.1 above, the IRR of the project is 20 per cent. So, in that example, optimal investment decisions could be made by comparing the project's IRR with the cost of capital in the case where the one-period cost of capital was constant over the life of the project: so long as the cost of capital was less than 20 per cent, the project should have been accepted. Matters are a little more complicated when the one-period cost of capital is not constant: in such circumstances the IRR must be compared with a constant cost of capital obtained either from a comparable financial asset which pays a fixed return over the same period of time as the lifetime of the project or from an appropriately weighted average of the one-period costs of capital.

Decisions simply to accept or reject an investment which are based on a comparison of the IRR with the cost of capital will be exactly equivalent to those based on the net present value rule whenever the net present value of an activity is a steadily declining function of the discount rate as in Fig. 2.1. In that diagram the net present value of the activity is zero at a discount rate r, which is therefore the activity's IRR. It is clear that, given the smooth decline of the activity's net present value as a function of the constant discount rate, the net present value of the activity is positive whenever the IRR exceeds the cost of capital, and negative when the IRR is less than the cost of capital.

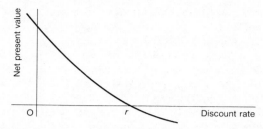

Fig. 2.1. The net present value of an activity as a function of the constant discount rate, with a unique internal rate of return

However, net present value cannot be guaranteed to be a steadily declining function of the discount rate. It is quite possible for the relationship to take the form shown in Fig. 2.2. Now there are two IRRs, r_1 and r_2. Net present value is positive at discount rates between r_1 and r_2, but negative otherwise. Hence if the cost of capital is less than r_1, the activity should not be undertaken, and thus investment decisions cannot be made simply by comparing the IRR and the cost of capital in this case. A situation like that depicted in Fig. 2.2 can arise when there is more than one change in the sign of the stream of net cash flows associated with an activity, as for example is the case whenever there are costs involved in shutting down a project so that both the initial net cash flow (the original cost of the investment) and the final one (the shut-down costs) are negative. If there is only one change of sign in the stream of net cash flows, with all negative ones preceding all positive ones, then the activity's net present value will be a steadily declining function of the constant discount rate and its IRR is guaranteed to be unique, so that investment decisions can be made using either the IRR or the net present value rule. We will assume henceforth that a unique IRR exists, although, for individual projects at least, this is rather restrictive.[4] As we shall see it is not a particularly restrictive assumption when applied to an evaluation of the performance of a firm or industry over a relatively short period.

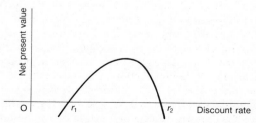

Fig. 2.2. The net present value of an activity as a function of the constant discount rate, with two internal rates of return

Even when the IRR is unique there is another complication which must be considered, and this is that the ranking of activities by IRR may differ from that given by net present value. Consider the example shown in Table 2.2. There are two activities, both of which require an initial investment of 100 at the end of period 0 and then generate positive net cash flows at the end of each of the next three periods. Activity 1 has the higher IRR, because it generates a large amount of cash at the end of period 1. But if the constant discount rate is 10 per cent then activity 2 has the higher net present value. If the interest in assessing activities is simply whether or not they should be undertaken then this problem does not matter: activities should be accepted if they have a positive net present value or, equivalently, if their IRR exceeds the cost of capital, and the ranking of activities which are going to be undertaken anyway is not relevant. But if activities are being assessed in order to see which is the most profitable (as is often the case in the comparison of firms or industries) then this problem does matter. If the activities are being assessed from an investor's point of view when credit is rationed and only a portion of desired investment can be undertaken, so that the issue is whether one project or firm yields higher returns than another, then the correct ranking is in terms of net present values (an activity with a higher net present value implies a larger increase in shareholder wealth), or, if the activities have different initial costs, in terms of net present value per unit of initial capital cost. If the activities are being assessed from a regulator's point of view then it is not clear what the correct ranking is; the regulator may be more concerned with the absolute size of the net present value generated by the activity than with net present value as a proportion of capital cost. Hence our discussion here is confined to the case where activities are assessed from an investor's viewpoint. So long as the returns to an investment accrue over several time periods, then the ranking by IRR can differ from the correct one. It is only if there is a single pay-off that the ranking by IRR will correspond with that by net present value, as can easily be checked from the definitions of net present value and IRR in equations 2.1 and 2.3. But physical investments which yield a single pay-off would appear to be rather rare, which implies that, in general, the IRR can be used only to indicate whether or not an activity should be undertaken (in conjunction with the cost

Table 2.2. Net cash flows, net present values (NPV), and internal rates of return (IRR) of two activities

| | Net cash flow by period | | | | | |
	0	1	2	3	IRR (%)	NPV at 10%
Activity 1	−100	102	14.4	8.64	20	11.12
Activity 2	−100	5.75	13.225	129.27	15	13.28

of capital) and not to indicate the relative profitability of different activities. We will return to this difficulty with the IRR in Chapter 3. It reflects the general problems of using the IRR to make correct investment decisions when the choices involve mutually exclusive activities.

Thus, if the stream of net cash flows associated with an investment changes sign only once, the decision as to whether or not an investment is (or was) justifiable can be made by comparing its IRR with the cost of capital. But unless the investment lasts for only one period, generating a single pay-off after the initial investment, the IRR cannot be used to compare the profitability of investment, as there is no guarantee that the ranking of investments which generate cash flows over several periods by IRR will correspond to that by net present value, which is the correct ranking. In general therefore the IRR of an investment, even when unique, can only be used to assess whether or not the investment should be (or should have been) undertaken.

2.2 Accounting profit rates

In many cases the data which are available for assessment of the performance of activities are accounting data which have been produced for rather different purposes. The traditional function of financial accounts is that of stewardship, and this role of accounts means that accounting data are primarily concerned with providing an objective picture of the way in which a firm has been run, for the benefit of the shareholders. The traditional accountant's view is that profitability is concerned with the assessment of the surplus of revenue over costs over some past period, usually the accounting year. Although accounting profits are primarily a historical statement of a company's record, the conventions which have developed in measuring accounting profits also affect forward-looking decisions: the decision as to whether or not to undertake an investment project is sometimes based on forecast accounting data.

The basic inputs into the computation of accounting profits are the net cash flows which, as we have seen, form the basis of optimal investment decisions. But a number of adjustments are made to these net cash flows to arrive at accounting profits, and these raise serious questions about the usefulness of such accounting data for assessing the performance of activities. One adjustment results from the accountant's desire to show profit as it is earned rather than when net cash flows are actually generated, so that the timing of actual net cash flows may differ from that of accounting profit figures. Secondly, an adjustment has to be made for costs that may not be directly associated with an individual project. Most obviously overhead costs may be allocated on an approximate pro rata basis across projects. However, the incremental overhead charge associated with a particular project may be very different from this allocation. The difference is that between marginal and average costs. In the case where the overhead is a fixed cost which a particular project does not augment, then no overhead should be attributed to the project in evaluating its incremental contribution to company performance. The most significant adjustment made by accountants to the net cash flow figures is that of depreciation charges. Accounts distinguish two sorts of cash outflows: current expenses and capital expenses. The former are deducted from cash inflows when accounting profits are computed but the latter are not. Instead, capital expenses are depreciated according to some more or less arbitrary rule[5] over a number of years, and the resulting annual depreciation charge is deducted from subsequent cash inflows in computing subsequent accounting profits. These depreciation decisions do not, of course, have any effect on cash flows,[6] and as a result accounting profit figures exclude some cash inflows.

The performance of an activity is often assessed on the basis of accounting data by means of the accounting rate of profit (ARP henceforth). This is defined as the ratio of the accounting profits earned in a particular period to the book value of the capital employed in the period. The book value of capital employed by an activity in a particular period is calculated by cumulating all the capital expenditures associated with the activity up to that period and subtracting all the depreciation charges up to that period from them. The ARP of an activity is thus computed on a very different basis from the IRR, not least in that it is calculated at a point in time rather than over the lifetime of the activity. The question naturally arises of what is the relationship between assessments of activities based on the comparison of the ARP with the cost of capital with those based on the comparison of the IRR with the cost of capital. An extensive literature has developed on the relationship between the ARP and the IRR, the conclusions of which are largely pessimistic and hence imply that the assessment of activities using the ARP may be highly misleading. Before considering this literature it will be useful to assess the investment project whose net cash flows were shown in Table 2.1 above on the basis of the ARP in order to illustrate the problems involved.

Table 2.3 shows the net cash flows of the project together with various

Table 2.3. Net cash flows and accounting profitability measures of a project

	Period				
	0	1	2	3	4
Net cash flow	−100	12	43.2	69.12	41.47
Accounting depreciation	—	25	25	25	25
Accounting profit	—	−13	18.2	44.12	16.47
Book value of capital at beginning of period	—	100	75	50	25
Accounting rate of profit (%)	—	−13	24.27	88.24	65.88

accounting measures. The project requires an initial cash outflow of £100 at the end of period 0, which is taken as equivalent to the beginning of period 1, and generates cash inflows at the end of each of the next four periods. The book value of capital employed in this project at the start of each period is given by the initial capital expenditure of £100 less cumulative depreciation charges up to that period. The depreciation charges are computed on a straight-line basis over the four periods, and the accounting profit figure in each period is given by subtracting the depreciation charge for the period from the cash inflow generated at the end of each period. The ARP in a period is measured as accounting profit in that period divided by the book value of capital employed at the beginning of the period.[7] As we know from the earlier discussion, this project has an IRR of 20 per cent, so that if the cost of capital per period is constant over time and less than 20 per cent the project is (or was) worth undertaking, while if the cost of capital per period is constant and greater than 20 per cent then the project is not (or was not) worth undertaking. However, it is not easy to see how an assessment of the project based on the ARPs in individual periods would reach the same conclusion as that based on its IRR. The ARP in period 1 is negative, and although in period 2 the ARP is relatively close to the IRR the ARPs in periods 3 and 4 vastly exceed the IRR. Faced with such variation in the project's ARPs it is not obvious what should be done in an attempt to measure its overall profitability: the natural first step of taking a simple average of the ARPs yields a figure of 41.35 per cent which is more than double the IRR. Clearly any assessment of the project based on the comparison of this simple average of the ARPs with the cost of capital will be very misleading: the project will appear to be (have been) worthwhile at (constant) costs of capital of up to 40 per cent per period, which we know to be incorrect. If the project's accounting profits over its lifetime are averaged and expressed as a ratio of the average book value of capital employed, the resulting profitability figure is 26.32 per cent: this is clearly closer to the IRR, but is still significantly above it.

It is important to note that the problems involved in using the ARP to assess the performance of an investment illustrated in Table 2.3 arise from one particular feature of the accountant's method of measuring profitability, namely the use of more or less arbitrary depreciation charges in arriving at accounting profits and book value of capital employed. As we shall see it is this aspect of accounting practice which has been regarded as crucial in the literature on the relationship between the ARP and the IRR, to which we now turn.

2.3   Does the ARP provide any information about the IRR?

There have been many analyses of the relationship between the ARP and the IRR, and the conclusions of most of this work have resulted in a widely-held view that the ARP of a project or firm is a very bad indicator of its IRR.

According to this view, the failings of the ARP are not due to the measurement problems which arise in using accounting information to measure profitability, such as the absence of inflation adjustments or the failure to capitalize activities such as research and development and advertising in the accountant's definition of assets employed. Rather, the view is that there is a fundamental conceptual problem: the ARP, even in ideal conditions, will in general bear little relation to the IRR, as illustrated in Table 2.3 above.

The two pioneering analyses were those of Harcourt (1965) and Solomon (1966), which investigated the relationship between the ARP and the IRR for individual projects and balanced stocks of projects under alternative assumptions about depreciation policy, asset life and the growth of the asset stock. Harcourt concluded that 'as an indication of the realised rate of return, the accountant's rate of profit is greatly influenced by irrelevant factors, even under ideal conditions', while Solomon's view was that 'book yield [i.e. ARP] is not an accurate measure of true yield [i.e. IRR]; the error in book yield is neither constant nor consistent'. A number of subsequent papers (Livingstone and Salamon (1970), Solomon (1970), Stauffer (1971)) reinforced the conclusions that the ARP was not an accurate measure of the IRR and that there was no systematic pattern in the discrepancies between the two which might have permitted corrections to be made to the ARP in order to arrive at a better indicator of the IRR. The view that the ARP provides no information about the IRR is now found in finance textbooks: for example Brealey and Myers (1981) state that 'book income [i.e. accounting profits] and ROI [i.e. ARP] are often seriously biased measures of true profitability and thus should not be directly compared to the opportunity cost of capital', and argue that managers should concentrate less on accounting measures of profitability and more on the net present value of projects or activities.

A paper by Fisher and McGowan (1983) provides a clear statement of the conventional scepticism as to the relevance of the ARP as a measure of the IRR. They prove a number of theoretical results (some of which were already known), applying to both pre- and post-tax ARPs, which we now list in summary form:

1. Unless the book value of capital employed by an investment is calculated as the present value of the remaining stream of cash flows associated with it discounted at the investment's IRR (note that the discount rate in this present value calculation is not in general the cost of capital), so that the depreciation charge in each period is the change in the present value so calculated, the ARP on a single investment will differ from period to period and will not in general equal the IRR in any period. If the ARP is constant over the project's lifetime then it equals the IRR. Thus the example in Table 2.3 illustrates a general point: unless a very special depreciation schedule is used (and one which is highly unlikely to occur in practice) the ARP will vary between periods and not in general equal the IRR in any one. Table 2.4 shows that if the

Table 2.4. Net cash flows and accounting profitability measures of a project when Hotelling depreciation is used

	Period				
	0	1	2	3	4
Net cash flows	−100	12	43.2	69.12	41.47
Hotelling depreciation		−8	21.6	51.84	34.56
Accounting profit (using Hotelling depreciation)		20	21.6	17.28	6.91
Book value of capital at beginning of period (using Hotelling depreciation)		100	108	86.4	34.56
Accounting rate of profit (%)		20	20	20	20

depreciation schedule used for the project we have been taking as an example calculates the depreciation charge in each period as the change in the present value of the project's remaining net cash flows discounted at its IRR of 20 per cent, a depreciation charge we call Hotelling depreciation (see Hotelling (1925)), the ARP in each period is constant and equal to the IRR. But Table 2.4 shows the exception rather than the rule: all other depreciation schedules will produce ARPs which vary and will not equal the IRR in any one period except by chance. In particular it should be noted that calculating the depreciation charge as the change in the present value of the project's remaining net cash flows discounted at the cost of capital, which is sometimes known as economic depreciation, will not in general produce a constant ARP equal to the IRR. The project's IRR must be known to calculate the depreciation schedule which makes its ARP constant and equal to the IRR.
2. The ARP for the firm as a whole is a weighted average of the ARPs for individual investments made in the past, with the weights being the book value of these past investments which depend on the depreciation schedule adopted and the amount and timing of such investments. It follows that the ARP for the firm as a whole will be constant only if one of two very special conditions holds: either the ARP on the firm's individual investments must be constant both over the lifetime of the investments and between investments, or the relative weights in the average must be constant over time. This latter condition in general requires that there should be a fixed proportion of investments with a given time pattern of returns in each year and that the firm should grow exponentially, increasing investment in each different type of asset by the same proportion each year. If the firm grows in this way it is said to be in steady-state growth.
3. Even when the firm does operate in the unrealistic manner of steady-state growth, so that its ARP is constant, the ARP varies with the rate of growth of the firm and will not generally equal the IRR. The only reliable inference that

can be made in the case of steady-state growth rate is that the ARP and the IRR will both be on the same side of the firm's steady-state growth rate: in particular this means that if the ARP equals the steady-state growth rate then it also equals the IRR. It is not true in general that the IRR for the firm must lie between the ARP and the steady-state growth rate, nor that the ARP of firms with high steady-state growth rates tends to understate their IRR while the ARP of firms with low steady-state growth rates tends to overstate their IRR.

On the basis of these theoretical results, together with some examples which show that the theoretical effects involved are far from being so small that they can be ignored in practice, Fisher and McGowan conclude that

there is no way in which one can look at accounting rates of return [i.e. ARPs] and infer anything about relative economic profitability or, *a fortiori*, about the presence or absence of monopoly . . . . The literature which supposedly relates concentration and economic profit rates [i.e. IRRs] does no such thing, and examination of absolute or relative accounting rates of return to draw conclusions about monopoly profits is a totally misleading enterprise.

This view reinforces Harcourt's original conclusion that

any 'man of words' who compares rates of profit of different industries, or of the same industry in different countries, and draws inferences from their magnitudes as to the relative profitability of investments in different uses or countries, does so at his own peril.

Put bluntly, the overall conclusion to be drawn from these studies would appear to be that the ARP provides no useful information for the purposes of economic analysis. It is such a bad indicator of the IRR that its use in any form of economic analysis is very questionable. The use of the ARP for any of the purposes discussed in Chapter 1—in empirical studies of industrial organization, for regulation of utilities and public enterprises, for investment appraisal, in competition policy, and in macroeconomic studies of profitability—would seem to be almost completely undermined. Before accepting this conclusion, however, it is necessary to analyse some aspects of the relationship between the ARP and the IRR in more detail.

2.4 The relationship between the ARP and the IRR over the complete lifetime of an activity

The impression conveyed by most of the existing literature on the relationship between the ARP and the IRR, as indicated in the previous section, is that very little can be said in general about this relationship. However, it is not true that there are no general results linking the ARP and IRR, and in this section we discuss those that are available for the case when the accounting profitability data cover the entire lifetime of the activity, in the sense that the data start and finish with a value of zero for the book value of capital employed. These results apply to both *ex ante* and *ex post* assessment of the activity, so to simplify the discussion and avoid the need to distinguish these two forms of assessment we shall again assume perfect certainty.

The relationship between the accountant's definition of profit in a period and the change in the book value of capital employed over the period is crucial in establishing general results linking the ARP and IRR, as has been emphasized by Peasnell (1982) and Franks and Hodges (1983). In the examples shown in Tables 2.3 and 2.4 above, accounting profit in a period was obtained from net cash flow in that period by deducting a depreciation charge, and the depreciation charge was equal to the difference between the book value of capital employed at the beginning of the period and the book value of capital at the end of the period. It will be assumed that this relationship between accounting profit, net cash flow, depreciation, and book value of capital employed always holds: formally we assume that

$$Y_t = F_t - K_t + (V_t - V_{t-1}) \qquad (2.4)$$

where Y_t is accounting profit in period t, F_t is revenue generated in t, K_t is new capital required in t, V_{t-1} is the book value of capital employed at the end of period $t-1$ (i.e. at the start of period t), and V_t is the book value of capital at the end of period t. Note that V_t, the book value of capital employed at the end of period t (or start of period $t+1$), is defined to include K_t, the new capital injected into the activity in period t. Accounting profit is obtained by subtracting a depreciation charge from revenue generated in t: equation 2.4 therefore implies that the depreciation charge in t, D_t, must be defined as

$$D_t = V_{t-1} - (V_t - K_t)$$

i.e. depreciation in t equals the change in the book value of capital employed between the beginning of t and the beginning of $t+1$, adjusted for any new capital required during t. The crucial feature of the relationship shown in equation 2.4 is that it requires *all* changes in the book value of capital employed to flow through the profit and loss account: the balance sheet and the profit and loss account are thus fully articulated. Given this assumption the following results linking the IRR of an investment and its ARP in each of the individual periods of its life can be obtained (the results are derived formally in the appendix to this chapter):

1. If the ARP over the investment's lifetime is constant then it equals the IRR, as we already know from the discussion of Fisher and McGowan's results. We also know from that discussion that the ARP will be constant over the lifetime of an investment only if the accounting depreciation schedule calculates depreciation in any period as the change over the period in the present value of the investment's subsequent net cash flows discounted at the investment's IRR, so that in practice it is most unlikely that an investment will have a constant ARP over its lifetime. This result is nevertheless of some practical

value. First it shows that the common practice in the case of non-competitive government contracts of paying the firm a constant ARP on the book value of the capital employed on government work will ensure that the IRR earned on such a project equals the constant ARP. This follows whatever depreciation scheme the firm employs: it can over-depreciate relative to Hotelling depreciation, but the consequence is that its capital base is reduced for the purpose of subsequent calculations by an exactly offsetting amount. Secondly it shows that if regulatory agencies use a constant ARP to assess the fair rate of return for regulated utilities, then a regulated firm earning accounting profits in line with the fair rate of return so determined will have an IRR equal to the constant ARP. These arguments can be generalized to the case where the ARP on government contracts, or used to determine the fair rate of return for a regulated utility, is varied over time in order to keep it in line with prevailing yields being earned in other activities. In this situation the firms involved will receive payments such that the present value of all receipts and expenditures, discounted at rates which are appropriate given the yields being earned elsewhere at the time, will be zero, and this will be true whatever depreciation scheme the firms use.

2. Consider two activities with different sequences of ARPs over their lifetimes. Suppose that it is possible to find some constant such that one activity always has ARPs greater than this constant while the other activity always has ARPs less than it. If this is the case then it follows that the activity which always has ARPs in excess of the constant has an IRR which is greater than that of the activity with ARPs consistently less than this constant. In particular if this constant is the cost of capital then an activity which always has ARPs in excess of the cost of capital has an IRR greater than the cost of capital, and conversely if the ARPs are always less than the cost of capital.

3. If the average accounting rate of profit over the life of an activity is defined as a weighted average of the individual ARPs with the weights being the book value of capital employed discounted at the cost of capital, then this average ARP will be greater than, equal to, or less than the cost of capital according as the IRR is greater than, equal to, or less than the cost of capital. A particular case of this result is that the IRR is equal to the average ARP of an activity weighted by the book value of capital employed discounted at the IRR, thus enabling the IRR of an activity to be derived iteratively from the ARPs and book values of capital employed over the activity's lifetime. Although proofs of all these results are contained in the appendix, it is useful to derive this final one in the attractively simple manner of Franks and Hodges (1983). Suppose that all cash flows occur at the ends of accounting periods. The IRR of an activity, r, is defined by the equation

$$-K_0 + \frac{F_1 - K_1}{(1+r)} + \frac{F_2 - K_2}{(1+r)^2} + \ldots + \frac{F_T - K_T}{(1+r)^T} = 0 \qquad (2.5)$$

If the initial book value V_0 is equal to K_0 and the ARP in the period ending at t,

a_t, is defined by

$$a_t = Y_t/V_{t-1} \qquad (2.6)$$

then equations 2.4 and 2.6 can be substituted into 2.5 and the resulting equation rearranged to give

$$\sum_{t=1}^{T} \left[\frac{a_t V_{t-1}}{(1+r)^t} - \frac{r V_{t-1}}{(1+r)^t} \right] = 0$$

so that

$$r = \frac{\displaystyle\sum_{t=1}^{T} \frac{a_t V_{t-1}}{(1+r)^t}}{\displaystyle\sum_{t=1}^{T} \frac{V_{t-1}}{(1+r)^t}} \qquad (2.7)$$

Equation 2.7 shows how the IRR can be computed iteratively from ARPs and book values of capital over an activity's lifetime.[8] The application of this technique to the project which has been used as an example throughout this chapter is illustrated in Table 2.5. If straight line depreciation is used in calculating accounting profit, the book value of capital employed and ARPs are as in Table 2.3, and suitably weighting these does indeed produce a figure of 20 per cent for the IRR.

Thus the IRR of an operation can always be found from accounting data if details of the ARP and book value of capital employed are available for every period of the operation's life. But although these results make it clear that general relationships between the IRR and the ARP do exist, their importance should not be overstated. One reason for this is that if book values and ARPs

Table 2.5. Example of calculation of a project's IRR from its suitably weighted ARPs and book values of capital

	Period			
	1	2	3	4
ARP (a_t)	−0.13	0.2427	0.8824	0.6588
Book value of capital employed at the beginning of the period (V_{t-1})	100	75	50	25
$a_t V_{t-1}/(1+r)^t$ ($r=0.2$)	−10.83	12.64	25.53	7.94
$V_{t-1}/(1+r)^t$ ($r=0.2$)	83.33	52.08	28.94	12.06

$\displaystyle\sum_{t=1}^{4} a_t V_{t-1}/(1+r)^t = 35.28 \qquad \sum_{t=1}^{4} V_{t-1}/(1+r)^t = 176.41 \qquad 35.28/176.41 = 0.20$

are known for the entire lifetime of an operation and the depreciation schedule is such that all changes in book value flow through the profit and loss account, then sufficient information is available for the net cash flows of the operation to be calculated, and hence it is possible to measure the operation's IRR directly. Substituting equation 2.6 into equation 2.4 shows that:

$$a_t V_{t-1} - (V_t - V_{t-1}) = F_t - K_t$$

Thus the conditions under which the IRR can be calculated from a weighted average of the operation's ARPs are also the conditions under which the ARPs and book values can be unscrambled to reveal the operation's net cash flows. This observation is, of course, merely a restatement of the fact that appropriately defined accounting rates of profit do provide economically relevant information in the single project case. It does not therefore detract from the contention that accounting profitability data can be of direct economic significance.

Another, more important, reason for caution in interpreting these results is that they apply only to sequences of accounting data which begin and end with values of zero for the book value of capital employed and cover a complete self-contained set of cash flows. The results are therefore useful for the assessment of the performance of a single investment project, but are much less so for evaluating the performance of firms or industries, as pointed out by Wright (1978). The results described above show that the IRR of a now defunct firm or industry can be calculated from accounting data, but this is an exercise of rather limited interest. It may be possible to apply the results to a continuing firm or industry by forecasting all its future ARPs and book values, but one then has to face the fact that firms and industries are generally rather long-lived investments, while the IRR is defined as a single figure irrespective of the duration of the investment. The relevance for any present purpose of a single rate of profit representing the overall performance of a currently operating firm which was founded in, say, 1900 is not obvious. In many cases interest focuses on the performance of a continuing firm or industry over a relatively short period of time, and in such circumstances the results described in this section are not directly applicable. It is to this more substantial issue that the next chapter therefore turns.

2.5 Conclusion

This chapter has provided the setting for an economic evaluation of accounting profitability figures. At the heart of the discussion lies the proposition that information on performance is of relevance in assessing investment decisions—either in an *ex ante* sense of whether the investment should be undertaken or in an *ex post* context of whether past investment decisions have been successful.

Two alternative techniques for evaluating investments have been suggested:

net present value and internal rates of return. The latter suffers from the difficulty that the IRR may not be uniquely defined. Furthermore if it is necessary to rank projects, perhaps because investment funds are limited, then NPV and IRR do not necessarily produce equivalent rankings. For most purposes NPV (perhaps defined as a proportion of initial capital costs) is the appropriate basis of assessment.

Even dismissing these problems associated with IRRs, a more fundamental difficulty arises in using accounting data for investment appraisal. A number of authors have noted that it is only in an exceptional circumstance that the ARP will equal the IRR. The exception is when the accounting depreciation charge used in the calculation of accounting profit is computed along the lines described by Hotelling as the change in the present value of remaining net cash flows discounted at the IRR. But in this case the IRR must already be known! Even the change in economic valuation, defined by using the cost of capital instead of the IRR to discount remaining net cash flows, will not yield a depreciation figure such that the ARP equals the IRR.

Much of the economics literature is therefore very pessimistic about the applicability of accounting information to economic analysis. The last section of this chapter demonstrated that this pessimism is exaggerated. At least in the single project case in which a complete set of accounting data is available for the entire life of the project then a number of valuable results are readily available:

1. If the ARP is constant for a single project then it equals the IRR.
2. If the ARP of one project is always in excess of the ARP of another then the IRR of the former is also in excess of the IRR of the latter.
3. If the ARP of a project is in excess of the cost of capital then so too is its IRR.
4. A weighted average ARP can be defined such that the IRR of the project is exactly equal to this average ARP.

Thus the IRR can be precisely derived from accounting information for a single project—a result that stands in marked contrast to the pessimism described in Section 2.3. However, for the very reason that the single project requires complete data over the entire life of the project, these results are only of limited interest. Of much more fundamental concern is the performance of a firm over a limited segment of its life. We pursue this line of argument in detail in the next chapter.

Notes

1. Hirshleifer (1958) is the classic reference, but there are also numerous textbook treatments, for example those by Brealey and Myers (1981) and (at a more rigorous level) Fama and Miller (1972).
2. Throughout this discussion we abstract from the difficulties associated with

disagreements amongst shareholders about the appropriate policy for the firm to follow. These can arise in the presence of uncertainty when the set of returns on an investment is not spanned by existing securities.

3. The major exceptions occur when a choice has to be made between mutually exclusive projects: even in this case the appropriate rule is to select projects in order of their net present value per unit of initial cost if capital is rationed in only one period.

4. For a more extensive discussion of this point see Flemming and Wright (1971).

5. There are a number of standard accounting depreciation methods: for example the straight-line method, where each year a constant proportion of the asset's depreciable value is deducted, the declining balance method, and the sum of the year's digits method.

6. Except in those cases where the accounting depreciation method used has consequences for tax and hence cash flows.

7. Other definitions of the ARP are clearly possible, for example accounting profit in a period could be divided by a simple average of the beginning- and end-period book values of capital employed, but the general features of the example do not depend on the precise definition of the ARP.

8. Computing the IRR iteratively using equation 2.7 involves picking a value for r, calculating the numerator and denominator of the ratio on the right-hand side of 2.7 from the accounting profitability data for the project's lifetime, evaluating the ratio and hence the implied value of r, recalculating the numerator and denominator of the ratio on the right-hand side of 2.7 with a new value of r, and continuing until the value of r implied by the ratio in equation 2.7 is consistent with the value of r used to calculate numerator and denominator of the ratio.

APPENDIX

In this appendix a number of propositions discussed in the text concerning the relationship between the ARP and IRR for a complete self-contained set of cash flows are proved using a continuous time framework.

Define $F(t)$ as the revenue generated by an activity at time t and $K(t)$ as the new capital required at that date. Accounting depreciation at t is an arbitrary amount $D(t)$ which yields a book value of capital employed $V(t)$ defined by

$$\dot{V}(t) = K(t) - D(t) \qquad (A2.1)$$

with $V(0)$ and $V(\infty)$ conventionally set at zero so that the whole life of the activity is covered ($\dot{V}(t)$ is the derivative of $V(t)$ with respect to time). The ARP at t is then defined as

$$a(t) = \frac{F(t) - D(t)}{V(t)} \qquad (A2.2)$$

and the IRR of the activity by r such that

$$\int_0^\infty \{F(t) - K(t)\}e^{-rt}\,dt = 0.$$

Attention is confined to activities with unique IRRs, so that

$$\frac{d}{di}\int_0^\infty \{F(t) - K(t)\}e^{-it}\,dt < 0 \ \forall\, i > 0. \tag{A2.3}$$

From equations A2.1 and A2.2

$$\dot{V}(t) - a(t)V(t) + F(t) - K(t) = 0 \tag{A2.4}$$

and hence

$$\int_0^\infty \{\dot{V}(t) - a(t)V(t)\}e^{-it}\,dt + \int_0^\infty \{F(t) - K(t)\}e^{-it}\,dt = 0.$$

Integrating this by parts gives

$$\int_0^\infty \{(i - a(t))V(t)\}e^{-it}\,dt + \int_0^\infty \{F(t) - K(t)\}e^{-it}\,dt = 0 \tag{A2.5}$$

which holds for any arbitrary value of i.

The following propositions can all be obtained by immediate application of equations A2.3 and A2.5:

Proposition 1: If a is constant then $r = a$

Proposition 2: Consider two activities with ARP profiles $a_1(t)$ and $a_2(t)$ respectively. Then if there exists some i such that $a_1 > i\,\forall\,t$ and $a_2 < i\,\forall\,t$, $r_1 > r_2$

One value of i which is of particular interest is the cost of capital ρ.

Proposition 3: If $a(t) \gtreqless \rho\,\forall\,t$ then $r \gtreqless \rho$.

Defining the average ARP over the life of the activity ($\bar{a}$) as

$$\bar{a} = \frac{\displaystyle\int_0^\infty a(t)V(t)e^{-\rho t}\,dt}{\displaystyle\int_0^\infty V(t)e^{-\rho t}\,dt}$$

then

Proposition 4: $\bar{a} \gtreqless \rho$ as $r \gtreqless \rho$.

The relationship between the activity's IRR and accounting data is given by

Proposition 5:
$$r = \frac{\displaystyle\int_0^\infty a(t)V(t)e^{-rt}\,dt}{\displaystyle\int_0^\infty V(t)e^{-rt}\,dt}$$

Proposition 1 can be generalized to the case where the ARP varies over time. The concept of the IRR can be generalized by noting that there are infinitely many valuation functions $q(t)$ such that

$$\int_0^\infty F(t)q(t)\,dt = \int_0^\infty K(t)q(t)\,dt.$$

Any such function is defined by a sequence of rates of return $r(t)$ and the conditions

$$q(0)=1,\ \dot{q}(t)=-r(t)q(t).$$

The IRR describes that particular valuation function for which $r(t)$ is constant. In general we can derive

Proposition 6: Every sequence of ARPs defines a valuation function under which the present value of the activity's cash flows is zero.

From (A2.4)

$$\int_0^\infty F(t)\exp\left[-\int_0^t a(x)\,dx\right]dt = \int_0^\infty a(t)V(t)\exp\left[-\int_0^t a(x)\,dx\right]dt$$

$$-\int_0^\infty \dot{V}(t)\exp\left[-\int_0^t a(x)\,dx\right]dt$$

$$+\int_0^\infty K(t)\exp\left[-\int_0^t a(x)\,dx\right]dt.$$

Integrating by parts gives

$$\int_0^\infty F(t)\exp\left[-\int_0^t a(x)\,dx\right]dt = \int_0^\infty K(t)\exp\left[-\int_0^t a(x)\,dx\right]dt$$

and $q(t)=\exp[-\int_0^t a(x)\,dx]$ has the properties $q(0)=1$ and $\dot{q}(t)=-a(t)q(t)$; hence $a(t)$ defines an appropriate valuation function.

3

The Value-to-the-Owner Rules for Capital Valuation

3.1 Introduction

THE analysis in the previous chapter showed that if the accounting data for an activity satisfied the condition that all changes in the book value of capital employed from period to period flowed through the profit and loss account then the activity's internal rate of return (IRR)—the measure of the rate of profit which is generally regarded as the economically relevant one—could be deduced from accounting rates of profit (ARP) and book values of capital employed covering the entire life of the activity. This proposition is true irrespective of the type of depreciation scheme employed. However, in many cases a complete set of accounting profitability data for an activity will not be available, particularly where long-lived activities such as continuing firms and industries are being assessed. The question naturally arises, therefore, of whether accounting profitability data covering only a relatively short segment of an activity's lifetime can provide any information about its IRR.

As Section 3.2 of this chapter demonstrates, the problem of relating ARPs to IRRs over a short segment is that opening and closing book values of the capital stock differ from those obtained by discounting subsequent cash flows at the IRR—the Hotelling valuation of capital. To be able to infer an activity's IRR from an isolated segment of its life, the excluded portions must be summarized in measures that value cash flows at the appropriate discount rate—namely the IRR. As Section 3.2 shows, certain relations between the ARP and IRR can be derived in the special case in which the activity is in steady state growth. But it is not possible to derive general relations between the ARP and IRR. Indeed it is not usually possible even to establish that the ARP will be greater than, less than, or equal to the IRR.

Of course this is really a restatement of the pessimism expressed in Section 2.3 of the previous chapter. But by focusing attention on the opening and closing valuations of capital employed, Section 3.2 serves to emphasize the issue that lies at the heart of the debate on the relevance of accounting profitability. If the book value of capital employed differs from the Hotelling valuation then the ARP will not equal the IRR. The importance of this result depends, however, on whether knowledge of an activity's IRR is useful. Clearly if the activity in question is a single investment project, then its IRR does provide useful information (subject to the qualifications discussed in

Section 2.1 of the previous chapter). But if the activity in question has a very long life (for example a continuing firm) then it is not obvious what meaningful information is provided by the IRR. The point here is that the IRR is defined as a single figure irrespective of the lifetime of an activity, so that it cannot be used to evaluate performance over a portion of an activity's life. For a firm which began life in 1930 and will continue until well into the next century, accounting data over the period 1970–86 will almost certainly not be useful in calculating its IRR, which depends on its lifetime net cash flows. But it is not clear what we could do with this figure even if we could deduce it from accounting data for 1970–86: our interest in the accounting data for this period is far more likely to stem from a desire to know whether the firm had performed well or badly over this period, and for this purpose the firm's IRR, which of course depends on its operations over a much longer time-span, is of questionable relevance. All of the criticisms of the usefulness of accounting profitability for economic analysis described in Section 2.3 of the previous chapter take it for granted that the ultimate test of the relevance of accounting data is whether an activity's IRR can be obtained from them. But if the IRR does not provide any meaningful information then the relevance of accounting measures of performance is being judged by the wrong yardstick.

What are the questions to which investors, economists, regulators, and others are seeking answers when they turn to accounts and other measures of performance? The previous chapter suggested one group of questions concerned with investment appraisal. Should a particular investment project or group of projects be undertaken? Another set of questions is concerned with retrospective evaluation. How well has the management of a firm done? In most of these cases interest centres on the evaluation of performance over a limited period, and hence the IRR cannot help with such an evaluation. Consequently the widespread pessimism about the relevance of accounting profitability information for economic analysis seems to us to be based on a misplaced view as to the usefulness of the IRR for evaluating an activity's performance.

In this and the following chapter we therefore explore the question of whether there exists an accounting profitability measure and an associated set of accounting valuation conventions that permit these economically relevant issues relating to an activity's performance over a segment of its lifetime to be addressed. We begin in Section 3.3 of this chapter by defining an accounting profitability measure over a finite segment of the life of an activity. This accounting rate of return (ARR) is the rate of return that discounts cash flows, including the terminal book value of capital employed, back to the initial book value of capital. It is the obvious counterpart to the IRR for a segment of an activity's life.

The value of the ARR will be crucially dependent on the opening and closing valuations of the capital stock. In Section 3.4 we discuss some accounting valuation concepts which have been widely advocated. 'Value-to-the-owner' rules have received a strong measure of support from both the accounting and academic professions, although a number of practical objections have been raised, as described in Section 3.5. While these valuation conventions are intuitively attractive, a theoretical rationale for their application has not yet been forthcoming. Chapter 4 and the remainder of the book is devoted to providing just such a rationale by demonstrating that if these valuation rules are adhered to, then the ARR computed using them provides meaningful answers to the various questions listed above.

3.2 The relationship between the ARP and the IRR over a segment of the lifetime of an activity

We begin the analysis of accounting profitability data which do not cover the complete lifetime of an activity by continuing the approach of the previous chapter, in which the relationship of ARPs to an activity's IRR was examined. Thus we are concerned with the question of whether accounting data covering only part of the activity's lifetime, and hence having at least one, and generally both, of the initial and final book values of capital employed different from zero, provide any information about the activity's IRR over its lifetime.

Maintaining the assumption that all cash flows occur at the end of a period, the IRR over an activity's lifetime can be defined in terms of a segment of its life lasting from the end of period 0 to the end of period T as

$$-M_0 + \frac{F_1 - K_1}{(1+r)} + \frac{F_2 - K_2}{(1+r)^2} + \ldots + \frac{F_T - K_T + M_T}{(1+r)^T} = 0 \tag{3.1}$$

where M_0 denotes the value of the activity at the end of period 0 (equivalent to the beginning of period 1) obtained by discounting all subsequent net cash flows back to the end of period 0 at the activity's IRR, and similarly for M_T, F_t is revenue generated in t, and K_t is new capital required in t. Substituting equations 2.4 and 2.6 into equation 3.1, adding and subtracting V_0 (the book value of capital employed at the end of period 0), and rearranging gives the following expression for the IRR (r):

$$r = \frac{\displaystyle\sum_{t=1}^{T} \frac{a_t V_{t-1}}{(1+r)^t} + (V_0 - M_0) - \frac{[V_T - M_T]}{(1+r)^T}}{\displaystyle\sum_{t=1}^{T} \frac{V_{t-1}}{(1+r)^t}} \tag{3.2}$$

where V_{t-1} denotes the book value of capital employed at the end of period $t-1$ (i.e. at the start of period t). Equation 3.2 makes it clear that if accounting data covering a segment of a continuing activity's life are to be used to deduce the activity's lifetime IRR, then it is necessary to make corrections for possible differences between book values of capital employed at the beginning and end of the segment under consideration and the corresponding values given by discounting subsequent net cash flows at the activity's IRR. Valuation errors of this sort over the intermediate period are irrelevant so long as all changes in book values flow through the profit and loss account in the manner of equation 2.4.

It is useful to examine the bias in the ARP as a measure of an activity's lifetime IRR when the available accounting data cover only a single period, and to do this we draw on the analysis of Franks and Hodges (1983). Consider the single time period from $t = 0$ to $t = 1$ and again assume that cash flows occur at the end of the period. The IRR of an activity over its lifetime is defined in terms of this single time period as

$$-M_0 + \frac{F_1 - K_1 + M_1}{1 + r} = 0$$

and this equation can be rearranged to give

$$r = \frac{F_1 - K_1}{M_0} + g_m \tag{3.3}$$

where $g_m = (M_1 - M_0)/M_0$ and is the rate of growth over the period of the value of the activity obtained by discounting subsequent net cash flows at the activity's IRR. Recalling equation 2.6, equation 2.4 becomes for this period

$$a_1 V_0 = F_1 - K_1 + V_1 - V_0$$

which gives on rearrangement

$$a_1 = \frac{F_1 - K_1}{V_0} + g_v \tag{3.4}$$

where $g_v = (V_1 - V_0)/V_0$ and is the rate of growth of book value over the period. Subtracting equation 3.3 from 3.4 gives an expression for the bias between the activity's ARP in this period and its IRR:

$$a_1 - r = (g_v - g_m) + \frac{F_1 - K_1}{M_0} \left[\frac{M_0}{V_0} - 1 \right]. \tag{3.5}$$

It is clear from equation 3.5 that the ARP can either exceed or fall short of the IRR, which is of course unsurprising in the light of the discussion in Section 2.3. Even if we suppose that the net cash flow at the end of period 1 is positive and the accountant's principle of conservatism implies that $M_0 > V_0$ so that the second term on the right-hand side of equation 3.5 is positive, it is quite possible for further over-depreciation during the period to result in g_v being less than g_m so that the first term on the right-hand side is negative and hence the sign of the bias is ambiguous.

Thus in order to deduce an activity's IRR from accounting data covering a short segment of its life, it is necessary to know how the activity's book value at the beginning and end of this segment relates to its value given by discounting subsequent net cash flows at its IRR. As knowledge of the activity's IRR is therefore essential in order to deduce the IRR from the ARP over short segments, there is obviously little point in performing this exercise. Accounting data covering a short segment of an activity's life cannot therefore provide any useful information about that activity's IRR. It is important to realize that the values that are required for comparison with book values will not in general be given by market values. Market values are given by discounting subsequent net cash flows at the cost of capital, not at the activity's IRR, and it is only when the activity's IRR equals the cost of capital that market values will be appropriate.

Using equation 3.3, equation 3.5 can be rearranged to express the relationship between the ARP in a single period and the IRR in a different way as follows:

$$a_1 - g_v = \frac{M_0}{V_0}(r - g_m).$$

If the activity is in a state of steady growth at the rate g then the ratio M/V and the ARP will both be constant over time, so that we have

$$a - g = \frac{M}{V}(r - g). \tag{3.6}$$

Equation 3.6 shows that in steady-state growth the ARP will equal the IRR only if $M = V$ or if $g = r$, and so confirms the claim made by Fisher and McGowan discussed in Section 2.3 that, if $M \neq V$, there is very little that can be said in general about the relationship between the ARP and the firm's steady-state growth rate of a given IRR. It is however clear from equation 3.6 that if the accountant's principle of conservatism succeeds in making M/V greater than one, then the IRR will lie between the ARP and the steady-state growth rate and the ARP of rapidly growing firms will understate their IRR (and conversely for slow growing firms).

3.3 The definition and measurement of the accounting rate of return

The discussion in the previous section was restricted to a single period analysis. Before we can make any further progress we have to define what is meant by an accounting measure of performance over a finite segment that spans a number of periods of cash flow. In examining a segment in the life of an activity we are concerned with the cash flows during that segment, but we must also take account of events which precede and succeed it. By treating the capital stock at the start of the segment as a purchase at that date, and the terminal capital stock as a sale, we can derive a complete series of cash flows from which a rate of return for the period taken as a whole can be calculated. Clearly such a rate of return will depend on the basis used for computing the values of the initial and terminal capital stocks, and we are interested in the interpretation of the rate of return which is obtained by using the book value of the firm's capital as a measure of capital input and output at the beginning and end of the segment respectively. We shall define this measure as the accounting rate of return (ARR). The ARR over a segment is that discount rate which makes the discounted value of the net cash flows over the segment plus the discounted book value of capital employed at the end of the segment equal to the book value of capital employed at the beginning of the segment. In formal terms the ARR over the segment from the end of period 0 to the end of period T is given by $\alpha_{0,T}$ such that

$$V_0 = \sum_{t=1}^{T} \frac{(F_t - K_t)}{(1+\alpha_{0,T})^t} + \frac{V_T}{(1+\alpha_{0,T})^T} \qquad (3.7)$$

where V_0 is the book value of capital employed at the end of period 0 (which is taken to be the same as the start of period 1), V_T is the book value of capital employed at the end of period T, F_t is revenue generated in t, K_t is new capital required in t, and all cash flows are assumed to occur at the end of the period.

Although the ARR over a segment is defined in terms of initial and terminal book values of capital and cash flows during the segment, the results of the previous chapter suggest that it can be deduced from accounting data provided that all changes in the book value of capital employed flow through the profit and loss account. This is indeed the case. If the accounting profit of the activity in period t, Y_t, is defined as

$$Y_t = F_t - K_t + V_t - V_{t-1} \qquad (3.8)$$

(which implies that depreciation in period t, D_t, equals $-[(V_t - K_t) - V_{t-1}]$) and the activity's accounting rate of profit in period t is

$$a_t = \frac{Y_t}{V_{t-1}} \qquad (3.9)$$

then, substituting equations 3.8 and 3.9 in 3.7 and rearranging, we find that

$$\alpha_{0,T} = \frac{\displaystyle\sum_{t=1}^{T} \frac{a_t V_{t-1}}{(1+\alpha_{0,T})^t}}{\displaystyle\sum_{t=1}^{T} \frac{V_{t-1}}{(1+\alpha_{0,T})^t}}. \qquad (3.10)$$

Equation 3.10 shows that, just as in the case discussed in the previous chapter where accounting data for the entire lifetime of an activity were available, the ARR over a segment of an activity's life can be calculated as a weighted average of the ARPs of the activity in the individual periods of the segment, where the weights are the book values of capital employed in each period discounted at the ARR. Hence if data on the activity's ARP and book value of capital employed are available for a number of periods the activity's ARR over that segment of its life can be calculated from the data iteratively. Notice that, if equation 3.8 holds, the ARP for period t (a_t) equals the ARR over the one-period segment from period $t-1$ to period t $(\alpha_{t-1,t})$. There are a number of advantages in focusing attention on the ARR over a one-period segment, apart from the computational one of not having to calculate the ARR iteratively on the basis of equation 3.10. One is that it is most straightforward to obtain costs of capital required for comparison with the ARR on a one year basis. Another is that the problem of possible non-uniqueness of the ARR (which arises for the same reasons as the non-uniqueness of the internal rate of return discussed in the previous chapter) is minimized by looking at a single year at a time, for then the opportunity for multiple sign changes in the stream of initial book value, cash flows, and final book value does not arise (assuming that both initial and final book value of capital employed are positive).

These ideas are illustrated by the simple numerical example in Table 3.1, which shows a three-period segment of the life of an activity with an initial book value of capital employed of 1,000 and a terminal book value of capital of 931.7. The activity's ARR over this segment is 10 per cent, as can be checked from the cash flows and initial and terminal book values of capital:

$$-1000 + \frac{150-40}{1.1} + \frac{161-40}{(1.1)^2} + \frac{133.1+931.7}{(1.1)^3} = 0.$$

Information about the activity's cash flows is of course unlikely to be available, but if the ARPs and book values of capital employed in individual periods are available this is enough to deduce the ARR. In the example,

$$\sum_{t=1}^{3} \frac{a_t V_{t-1}}{(1.1)^t} = 240.87 \text{ and } \sum_{t=1}^{3} \frac{V_{t-1}}{(1.1)^t} = 2408.7,$$

confirming that a suitably weighted average of the individual ARPs will reveal the ARR to be 10 per cent.

3.4 Accounting valuation conventions

It is clear that the interpretation of the ARR will depend on the accounting conventions used to establish the initial and terminal book values of capital

Table 3.1. A segment of the life of an activity

Period	V_{t-1}	V_t	Depreciation $(= -[(V_t - K_t) - V_{t-1}])$	F_t	K_t	$Y_t (= a_t V_{t-1})$	a_t
1	1000	960	80	150	40	70	0.07
2	960	940	40	161	40	101	0.1052
3	940	931.7	58.3	183.1	50	124.8	0.1328

employed. Accounting theory offers a number of different valuation concepts, and we do not intend to discuss them in any detail (Whittington (1983) gives an excellent discussion of the relative merits of each of the major valuation bases). The valuation base of traditional accounting is historic cost, which is the depreciated original cost of assets. Accounts based on historic cost values are of some use, as records of past events, in fulfilling the traditional stewardship role of accounting. But if accounts are to provide information relevant to current decisions then it is current values, which represent the value of opportunities currently available, rather than historic cost ones, that are more likely to be useful.

As there are a number of opportunities open to a business at any moment there are correspondingly a number of current value bases available. One opportunity currently available is to replace assets, and this leads to the replacement cost valuation base (RC)—the current cost of purchasing similar assets.[1] Another is to sell assets, and this leads to the net realizable value base (NRV)—the disposal value of assets. A third opportunity is to continue to use assets, and this leads to the present value base (PV)—the present value of future net cash flows associated with current assets discounted at the cost of capital. The fact that several current value bases are available raises the problem of whether any single current valuation method should be chosen and, if so, which one. The case for each of these three broad bases has been made by a number of authors, and Whittington (1983) has given a comprehensive survey of the arguments for and against them. Whittington concludes that 'each is of potential relevance in particular circumstances', and hence it is natural to consider an approach to valuation which makes use of all three 'pure' current valuation bases, selecting according to their relative values for the assets concerned. This is the basis known variously as 'value-to-the-owner', 'opportunity value', or 'deprival value', which we shall refer to by the first of these names.

The basic method of the value-to-the-owner valuation technique is to choose one of RC, NRV, or PV as the value of an asset by establishing the minimum loss that a firm would suffer if it were deprived of an asset. The idea seems to originate from the USA in the 1920s. Canning (1929) devised rules of the value-to-the-owner type, and his work influenced that of Wright (1964 and 1970). Bonbright (1937) also devised rules of this form, and his work was explicitly acknowledged by Baxter (1967, 1971, and 1975), Edey (1974), Parker and Harcourt (1969), Solomons (1966) and Stamp (1971). In the UK, in 1975 the Sandilands Committee adopted value-to-the-owner (which it referred to as 'value to the business') as the appropriate valuation base in its report on inflation accounting. In the USA, value-to-the-owner rules for asset valuation were incorporated into the Financial Accounting Standards Board's 1978 Exposure Draft 'Financial Reporting and Changing Prices' and the subsequent 1979 Financial Accounting Standard of the same title. They were similarly incorporated in the 1979 Canadian Exposure Draft 'Current Cost

The Value-to-the-Owner Rules

Accounting' and the 1982 Canadian Standard 'Reporting the Effects of Changing Prices'. In Australia a simplified version of the value-to-the-owner rules, in which the amount of replacement cost recoverable from the further use of the asset ('recoverable amount') is substituted for present value,[2] was introduced in the 1976 Provisional Accounting Standard 'Current Cost Accounting' and eventually incorporated into the 1983 Statement of Accounting Practice No. 1 of the same title. This simplification was also incorporated both in the UK Exposure Draft 24 of 1979 (see Gibbs and Seward (1979)) and the subsequent Statement of Standard Accounting Practice 16 'Current Cost Accounting' of 1980, and in the New Zealand Exposure Draft 'Current Cost Accounting' of 1981 and the subsequent 'Current Cost Accounting Standard No. 1' of 1982.

The value-to-the-owner rules are commonly set out in inequality form, as in Table 3.2. There are six logically possible relationships between RC, NRV, and PV, and for each possible case there is a particular value which is the minimum loss that a firm would suffer if it were deprived of an asset: this is the value to the owner in that particular case. In each of cases 1, 2, 5, and 6 it would be worthwhile to replace the asset if the firm were deprived of it, so that in these cases replacement cost sets a ceiling on the loss that would be suffered. In cases 3 and 4 replacement is not worthwhile, and the value to the owner in these cases depends on which of two opportunities available, given that the asset is already owned by the firm, is more profitable—continued use (case 3) or disposal (case 4).

However although there are six logically possible relationships between RC, NRV, and PV, in practice 'for fixed assets, cases in which the asset's selling price (NRV) exceeds its buying price (RC) *are all likely to be extremely rare*' (Gee and Peasnell (1976)—emphasis in original). A situation in which NRV is greater than RC is unlikely to persist for long, for in these circumstances firms will be able to make a sure profit by selling the assets they possess and buying new ones which will lower selling price and raise buying price, and this process will continue until RC is no longer less than NRV. If it is assumed that RC is never less than NRV, then only cases 1, 3, and 4 in Table 3.2 need be considered. Under the assumption that $RC \geqslant NRV$, the value-to-the-owner

Table 3.2. Value-to-the-owner rules

Case	Relationship between RC, NRV, and PV	Value to the owner
1	$PV_t > RC_t > NRV_t$	RC_t
2	$PV_t > NRV_t > RC_t$	RC_t
3	$RC_t > PV_t > NRV_t$	PV_t
4	$RC_t > NRV_t > PV_t$	NRV_t
5	$NRV_t > PV_t > RC_t$	RC_t
6	$NRV_t > RC_t > PV_t$	RC_t

rules for asset valuation can be written as

$$V_t = \left.\begin{matrix} RC_t \\ PV_t \\ NRV_t \end{matrix}\right\} \quad \text{if} \quad \left\{\begin{matrix} PV_t > RC_t > NRV_t \\ RC_t \geqslant PV_t \geqslant NRV_t \\ RC_t > NRV_t > PV_t. \end{matrix}\right. \tag{3.11}$$

An equivalent way of formulating the value-to-the-owner rules is to define the economic value of an asset (EV) as the higher of PV or NRV—clearly if the value of an asset in current use (PV) is less than its disposal value (NRV) it is in the interests of a firm's shareholders for that asset to be sold, so that its economic value is NRV, while if PV > NRV it is in the shareholders' interests for the asset to be retained in use, making economic value equal to PV—and then say that value to the owner is given by the lower of replacement cost and economic value. Formally

$$V_t = \min\{RC_t, EV_t\} \quad \text{where} \quad EV_t = \max\{PV_t, NRV_t\}. \tag{3.12}$$

3.5 Objections to 'value-to-the-owner' rules

There are a number of difficulties involved in using the value-to-the-owner basis for valuation. At a conceptual level several authors have objected that there is no theoretical underpinning to the value-to-the-owner rules. Whittington (1983) concludes his discussion of the value-to-the-owner concept by saying that 'it is to some extent still a practical technique in search of a theoretical justification' and that it is necessary to know more about the properties of the income measure to which it gives rise. He regards the most fundamental problem with the concept as being that 'value to the owner has never been demonstrated to arise out of a particular information requirement of a potential user of financial reports, other than that of an insurer'. This criticism has also been made by one of the present authors in earlier work: Kay (1977) states that 'there are few . . . purposes [other than insurance] for which it is useful to know the loss which you would suffer if deprived of an asset'.

Chapter 4 is primarily devoted to providing the theoretical rationale for the value-to-the-owner rules. But in addition a number of practical objections have been raised, which can be classified under four headings: subjectivity, aggregation, intangibles, and capitalization. In considering these objections we can for the most part do no more than restate well documented practical difficulties, although in some cases the theoretical analysis of Chapter 4 sheds light on how these problems should be addressed. Hence at this stage we largely reserve comment on these issues until the next chapter, and merely document objections for future reference.

Subjectivity. The main practical objection which is raised against any form of current valuation is the subjectivity involved, in contrast to the objectivity of historic cost values which results from historic cost being based on the recording of events which have actually occurred (although it must be noted that the objectivity of the depreciation schemes used to establish historic cost values is open to question). As the value-to-the-owner rules combine each of the three pure valuation bases they unfortunately involve the subjectivity problems of all. Present value is the valuation base which suffers most severely from the difficulties of subjectivity, as it depends entirely upon estimates of future cash flows and discount rates. But replacement cost and net realizable value have similar, though less severe, problems. It is by no means straightforward to establish the net realizable value of a partly used asset which has a highly specialized function, although it is clear that for many assets difficulties of this sort will not arise. As for replacement cost it is necessary to specify what concept of replacement is involved: when technical progress or changes in relative prices have occurred there is a divergence between the cost of physical replacement of an asset and the cost of replacing the services yielded by the asset. When the two concepts of replacement cost differ this means that the assets currently used by the firm are not the best current practice ones: if it were to purchase the services yielded by its assets at their lowest current market price it would not buy those it is currently using. In our view the appropriate concept of replacement cost is the minimum cost of replacing the services yielded by the firm's existing assets: replacement cost valuation means valuing assets at the cost of replacing the services embodied in them. In assessing the cost of replacement of the service, an appropriate allowance must be made for any changes in the costs of other factors of production which are associated with replacement of the service by a physically different asset, which requires the estimated present value of these cost changes to be added to or subtracted from the cost of the new asset in calculating the replacement cost of existing assets. All three valuation bases thus have subjectivity problems, and value-to-the-owner has all of them. We do not have any simple solutions to these difficulties, and can only make the usual response in this situation that 'it is better to be roughly right than precisely wrong'. Current values are less precise than historic cost ones, but they are far more useful, as we shall demonstrate in what follows.

Aggregation. Another problem in applying the value-to-the-owner rules concerns aggregation. These rules have their roots in the valuation of individual assets, but the sum of the values to the owner of individual assets may, when the assets are interdependent, fail to indicate the value to the owner of the group of assets taken as a whole. Consider the example given by Edey (1974) where an electricity generating system comprises a number of coal-fired stations with a large-scale interconnected grid. The system as a whole is semi-obsolescent, but hypothetical replacement of one coal-fired station alone would not allow the complete reconstruction of the system as a whole, so that the replacement cost of a coal-fired station would be the cost of a similar station which would fit in with the rest of the system. The sum of the replacement costs of the components of this system would be much larger than the replacement cost of the system as a whole.

The above example of aggregation difficulties concerned technical progress, but aggregation problems can arise in other circumstances. In the presence of economies of scale or scope the sum of the replacement costs of the components of the system taken one by one can fall below the cost of replacing the system as a whole. If the replacement cost of a component is defined as the replacement cost of the whole less the replacement cost of all other components, then the marginal cost of the last component will fall below the average cost of the system. Likewise, economies of scale or scope cause the sum of economic values of components to exceed the economic value of the system. Here we define economic value of a component as the economic value of the system less the economic value of all other components. In the case of the electricity generating system, the presence of the fixed cost of the network and overhead charges of managing the system will cause the sum of replacement costs to fall short of the replacement cost of the system and the sum of economic values to exceed the economic value of the system. Thus if

$$RC(i) = RC\left(\sum_j j\right) - RC\left(\sum_{j \neq i} j\right) \tag{3.13}$$

and

$$EV(i) = EV\left(\sum_j j\right) - EV\left(\sum_{j \neq i} j\right) \tag{3.14}$$

where $RC(i)$ = replacement cost of asset i

$RC\left(\sum_j j\right)$ = replacement cost of the system

$EV(i)$ = economic value of asset i

$EV\left(\sum_j j\right)$ = economic value of the system

then in the presence of economies of scale or scope

$$\sum_i RC(i) < RC\left(\sum_j j\right) \text{ and } \sum_i EV(i) > EV\left(\sum_j j\right).$$

By itself the above does not raise particular difficulties. If the replacement of the electricity generating system as a whole is being considered then the relevant degree of aggregation is the system as a whole for replacement cost and economic value measurement. Thus $EV\left(\sum_j j\right)$ should be assessed in relation to $RC\left(\sum_j j\right)$ taking account of technological advances if replacement of the system as a whole permits their exploitation. If investment in a component is at issue then $RC(i)$ and $EV(i)$ are the relevant measures. Similarly we may be interested in evaluating performance either at the aggregate or at the individual component level. Accounting statements for firm groups provide information on performance at the aggregate level. However, managerial monitoring may require performance evaluation at subsidiary, plant or asset level.

The more troublesome question comes at the stage of asking whether the value-to-the-owner rules should be applied at the level of a group of assets or at individual component level. Thus abstracting for the moment from economies of scale or scope, is the value of the group of assets appropriately obtained as

$$\min\left(\sum_i RC(i), \sum_i EV(i) \right) \tag{3.15}$$

or

$$\sum_i \min(RC(i), EV(i))? \tag{3.16}$$

To take an example, one of the stations in the electricity generating system discussed above may, through being favourably located, have lower operating costs than the remainder. Its economic value may therefore exceed its replacement cost while economic value falls short of replacement cost for the other stations. Since equation 3.16 is always less than, or equal to equation 3.15, applying the value-to-the-owner rules at the individual asset level usually yields a lower accounting valuation of the capital stock. The accounting valuation is lower because in constructing its bundle of assets the firm is assumed to be able to combine judiciously assets already in place with opportunity costs $EV(i)$ and assets external to the firm with costs of employment of $RC(i)$. In equation 3.15 the firm is required to choose from a set of assets either external to the firm (with opportunity cost $\sum_i RC(i)$) or internal to the firm (with opportunity cost $\sum_i EV(i)$). In general, the cost of a set of assets assembled in the former way will be lower than the cost of a set obtained in the latter manner. In the presence of economies or diseconomies of scale or scope, the analysis is complicated by the interaction between assets in place in the firm and assets purchased externally. A simple minimum condition does not therefore apply. But the principle remains the same and the difference between applying the value-to-the-owner rules at the individual and aggregate level boils down to a question of whether components external and internal to the firm can be aggregated together, or whether the firm is faced with a choice of buying the system externally or retaining existing assets. We will see in the next chapter that the answer to the question depends on whether an *ex ante* investment appraisal or an *ex post* performance evaluation is being undertaken. In the case of an investment analysis, an expansion of operations by the purchase of additional assets is being contemplated. In a performance evaluation, the question of whether existing assets could be better organized is being addressed. In the former case, equation 3.15 is relevant and in the latter 3.16 applies. Accounting statements are *ex post* records so that equation 3.16 applies in practice. But it then has to be borne in mind that one of the reasons why adjustments have to be made in undertaking investment appraisals is that the opportunity set presented to the firm *ex ante* is not that which has been used in the *ex post* evaluation. This gives rise to an interesting distinction between performance and investment evaluations which differs from the normal marginal/average distinction i.e. equations 3.15 and 3.16 differ even in the absence of economies of scale and scope. We return to this in the next chapter.

Intangibles. One of the items that accountants have found most troublesome to evaluate has been intangible assets. Goodwill is usually considered under three headings:

(i) premia arising on consolidation of subsidiaries representing the excess of the cost of an acquisition over its book value,
(ii) rights or facilities such as production rights, processes or 'know-how' and premia paid for tangible assets in excess of their book value,
(iii) assets such as patents, trade-marks and copyrights.

The conflict between recording the historic cost of acquiring an asset and the current value to owners of assets in possession becomes most blatant in the case of assets for which no simple mechanical correction to the former permits the approximate derivation of the latter. It is therefore tempting to go to the other extreme of saying that goodwill is essentially the residual item that reconciles a market valuation of the firm with the book value of tangible items. According to this approach then, goodwill equals the market value of the firm less its book value of tangible items. The premia on consolidation of acquired assets is an example of an application of this latter approach. The other components of goodwill referred to above are frequently recorded on a cost basis and written off over a variety of periods thereby yielding a valuation that bears little relation to a market value.

The treatment of goodwill as the difference between market and book value may or may not be appropriate. Consider first the case of a proposed investment by an existing firm of high repute. Suppose that its reputation extends into the new market. In that case an important reason why the economic value of the investment may exceed its cost is that the cost of acquiring one of its constituent inputs, namely goodwill, is zero. For example, when Mercedes–Benz diversified into the smaller/medium sized saloon range its performance in that market reflected a reputation established elsewhere. Valuing the goodwill at its economic value would clearly be inappropriate and would erroneously eliminate the apparent desirability of the investment. The reason that it is profitable for Mercedes to diversify is that its cost of establishing a reputation in the new market is below that of other firms, i.e. there is an economy of scope. The value-to-the-owner rule of valuing goodwill at the minimum of replacement cost and economic value is again directly appropriate here.

What happens when at some future date we come to evaluate the performance of this investment? There are a number of questions that might be of interest in an *ex post* assessment and the next chapter discusses the differences in approach required to answer them. One issue that is of concern to investors is the performance of management. Here we are interested in whether another management (or, to be precise, the best alternative management) could have surpassed the performance of the existing management. Suppose that the new management could have replicated consumers' perceptions of the firm's reputation at some cost through the use of, for example, guarantees or advertising promotion.[3] Then we would expect that the economic value which the existing management could extract from its goodwill is this cost of replicating reputation. If economic value exceeds the replacement cost then the existing management can generate the stream of benefits associated with the goodwill at lower cost than the best alternative management. The current management is exploiting the asset goodwill to better advantage than others could and this is reflected in an economic value in excess of replacement cost. If the replacement cost of goodwill exceeds its economic value then goodwill is valued at economic value where this is, as before, determined as the difference between the economic value of the firm in the presence and absence of this asset. In that case, the cost of substituting an alternative management is not a replication cost (since this is too expensive to be worthwhile) but the economic value of the existing management's reputation itself. But even in this case in which goodwill is recorded at economic value, goodwill does not, in general, equal the difference between economic and book value. It is only if all component assets are valued at economic value and goodwill is determined likewise that this will be appropriate.

Capitalization. Separate from the question of the valuation of assets is the issue of which assets should be included in a measure of the firm's capital stock. By the replacement cost of the firm's capital it will be recalled that we mean the cost of acquiring capital assets that yield the stream of services that the firm is producing. Some of the services will only be produced in the future so that the issue of what items should be capitalized in the firm's assets and liabilities centres around a description of the future stream of services that we are attempting to replicate. At one extreme, market valuations capitalize the stream of all predictable future services, attribute certain probabilities to the realization of these services, and discount them at some appropriate risk-adjusted rate. At the other, accounts tend in the direction of only capitalizing services to which the firm (or its owners) has a property right or legal liability—assets in place. Definitions of goodwill referred to above included patents, trademarks, copyrights, selling or production rights but did not include promotion expenditure or measures of reputation. The 1981 Companies Act requires that research costs be written off as incurred.

Deferred taxation is designed to reconcile tax and accounting treatments of assets in place but not anticipated future investments. Marketable financial investments are valued at acquisition cost or market value and thus indirectly or directly refer to anticipated future investments while only current and past investments are recorded for consolidated subsidiaries. Dividends announced but not yet paid are capitalized but future anticipated dividends are not. Pension provisions are made for existing or past but not future services by employees. Work in progress but not in prospect is capitalized. Accounting valuation procedures display considerable variation across items but the principle of restricting accruals to current or past activities and future services to which a company has already established property rights is well established.

The distinction between forward-looking market valuations and backward-looking accounting valuations is an important one. The exclusion of future services over which a company has not yet established property rights is a useful benchmark for distinguishing *ex post* out-turns from *ex ante* prospects. Measuring performance in relation to market valuation will only reveal abnormal returns if *ex ante* expectations were not fulfilled. Measuring performance in terms of accounting valuations (even if stated at economic value and not replacement cost) will reveal abnormal returns if subsequent activities contribute to property claims at a rate that differs from the cost of capital. Irrespective of whether the earnings or liability was anticipated, if a claim materializes in a particular period, then accounting performance will be affected.

The property right concept would appear to be the appropriate one for distinguishing between assets and liabilities in place, and future opportunities. An accounting measure of performance should be able to provide information about the returns to investment decisions that may have been entirely predictable but are only currently being implemented as reflected in the receipt of a payment or the signing of a contract. Where a correct application of value-to-the-owner rules differs from the practices described above is in its valuation of assets in place. An expenditure on research and development or the training of the labour force may not yet have yielded a patent or a return on skills acquired but the expenditure has been made and if there is any prospect of a return being earned then that expenditure should not be capitalized at less than its economic value. If there is a strong possibility of a high profit accruing then the expenditure should not be valued at more than its current replacement cost. In other words, a consistent application of the rule that assets be valued at the minimum of replacement cost and economic value implies that an immediate write-off of such an expenditure is rarely appropriate.

Likewise a range of activities that are currently treated as 'off balance sheet' items should in general be accounted for. An option to purchase or sell an asset will have an economic value. Transaction costs will in general cause replacement cost and realizable value on disposal to lie on opposite sides of present value. Occasionally an informed assessment of present value will cause market values as reflected in replacement cost and disposal value to lie on one or other side of present value. Irrespective of whether such options are valued at replacement cost or economic value the fact that a contract has been signed giving the firm a future option means that this service should be capitalized. However, options that a firm is likely to sign in the future (which will be reflected in the firm's market value) are excluded from accounting valuations. Research and development expenditures that may follow naturally on from past expenditure will be captured in market but not accounting valuations. Where past operations and expenditures have given a firm a right to future services or an obligation to provide future services, then these should be valued. Existing conventions correctly attempt to distinguish between past and future activities but confuse these with the past and future earnings to which their activities are likely to give rise. It is appropriate to exclude future activities to which a firm is not yet obligated but incorrect to exclude the earnings and costs associated with future services deriving from past activities to which the firm is obligated.

3.6 Conclusion

The chapter began by arguing that in most circumstances the economist, investor, or regulator is interested in the performance of a firm over a limited segment of its life. The results of the previous chapter are not generally applicable to this type of analysis. Section 3.2, however, demonstrated that in steady state growth relations between the ARP and IRR can be derived. In particular if the accountant's principle of conservatism keeps the accounting valuation of assets below the value given by discounting future net cash flows at the IRR then the IRR will lie between the ARP and the steady-state growth rate and the ARPs of rapidly growing firms will understate their IRR.

Generally, for a limited segment of the life of a firm, accounting measures of performance will be affected by the conventions that are employed in valuing the opening and closing capital stock. Several accounting conventions have been suggested. The one that is discussed in some detail in this chapter is the value-to-the-owner rule by which the accounting valuation of the capital stock is equated to the lower of economic value and replacement cost. Economic value is in turn defined as the maximum of the present value of the expected future earnings of an asset and its net realizable value on disposal. Thus the value-to-the-owner rules set upper and lower bounds at replacement cost and disposal value around an asset's present value. The next chapter demonstrates that an application of value-to-the-owner rules permits a range of economically interesting questions about company and investment performance to be answered.

But before these questions can be considered, some of the practical difficulties associated with the implementation of these rules have to be addressed. Section 3.5 considered four of these: the subjectivity of replacement cost and economic valuations; the question of how the rules should be applied at the aggregate level of the plant, firm, or industry; the measurement of intangibles; and the issue of what should be included in the capital stock. On subjectivity, we argued that the difficulties inherent in establishing valuations do not undermine the validity of recording best estimates. On aggregation, it was suggested that in the *ex ante* appraisal of investment the value-to-the-owner rules should be applied at the aggregate level. In an *ex post* assessment of performance it may be appropriate to apply the rules at the individual asset level. Goodwill, it was argued, should be treated like any other asset and valued at the minimum of its replacement cost and economic value. Finally, the appropriate criterion by which assets should or should not be capitalized is not the degree of uncertainty attaching to future earnings and liabilities, but whether actions and decisions in the relevant time period establish legal claims to future services. Irrespective of the degree of uncertainty surrounding the value of these services, they should be capitalized at the minimum of replacement cost and economic value.

Notes

1. Exactly what is meant by 'similar assets' in the context of replacement is discussed below.
2. Recoverable amount requires the estimation of future cash flows, and so differs from present value only in that a discount rate is not applied to future cash flows.
3. Deferred managerial compensation (e.g. generous pension provisions, or a rising lifetime remuneration scheme) is one means by which a management could signal quality.

4

The Assessment of Activities over Limited Segments using Accounting Profitability Data

4.1 Introduction

CHAPTER 3 described a set of accounting valuation conventions, the value-to-the-owner rules, which have been suggested by several commentators to be an intuitively appealing compromise between the three current valuation bases, but for which no theoretical rationale has as yet been forthcoming. The purpose of this chapter is to demonstrate that the value-to-the-owner rules can be used to investigate economically interesting questions.

One set of questions concerns the desirability of undertaking a particular investment project. Section 4.2 of this chapter demonstrates that accounting profitability figures obtained using value-to-the-owner rules as the valuation convention can assist in an investment appraisal and in particular can indicate the desirability of undertaking, postponing, or not implementing an investment. Section 4.3 returns to the practical issue raised in Chapter 3 of the way in which assets should be aggregated for the purpose of making *ex ante* investment decisions.

Section 4.4 considers the *ex post* performance of assets in place. Accounts are used for a variety of *ex post* assessments. Investors are interested in the return that has been earned on equity funds invested in comparison with what could have been earned had a different management been in charge or different investment decisions been made. Regulators are interested in whether barriers to entry into or exit from an industry are indicated. Economists are concerned about how market structure has affected performance.

As Section 4.5 of this chapter shows, the *ex post* analysis of performance raises different problems of aggregation from the *ex ante* one. The difference arises from the wider range of opportunities presented by replication in the *ex post* case than in the *ex ante* one. Section 4.6 concludes this chapter.

4.2 The use of the ARR in making investment decisions

To demonstrate that if the book values of initial and terminal capital stocks are valued on value-to-the-owner conventions, the accounting rate of return (ARR) defined in the previous chapter is directly relevant to economic analysis, we first consider the use of the ARR in investment decisions. We wish to establish that if, at the beginning of a segment of the life of an activity, the expected ARR over the segment exceeds the cost of capital, then the activity should be undertaken at the start of the segment. On the other hand, if the expected ARR over the segment is less than the cost of capital, then the activity should not be undertaken at the start of the segment. The analysis is perfectly general, in that the activity in question might be a particular investment project or an entire firm, and hence the decision involved might be whether or not to undertake a particular project or whether to enter or leave a particular industry.

We use the simplest possible example to show that investment decisions can be correctly made by comparing the expected ARR of an activity with the cost of capital. It is assumed that the decision is being made at the end of period 0 (which we take to be equivalent to the beginning of period 1) and that the segment in question lasts for just one period, until the end of period 1. The cash flows in period 1 occur at the end of the period. We show in the appendix to this chapter that our conclusions about the relevance of the ARR based on value-to-the-owner conventions do not depend on the simple one-period nature of this example. The cash flows and the book value of capital at the end of period 1 are of course not known at the beginning of period 1. We use an asterisk to indicate the cash flows and book value of capital which, at the start of period 1, are expected to occur at the end of period 1. The expectations held at the beginning of period 1 are single-valued and held with certainty: under appropriate conditions they can be regarded as certainty equivalents.[1]

The expected ARR on value-to-the-owner conventions over period 1 is given by α^* where

$$V_0 = \frac{F_1^* - K_1^*}{1 + \alpha^*} + \frac{V_1^*}{1 + \alpha^*} \qquad (4.1)$$

and, for simplicity, the subscripts indicating the segment over which α^* is measured have been suppressed. In this equation F_1^* is the revenue generated at the end of period 1 which is expected at the end of period 0; K_1^* is the new capital required at the end of period 1 which is expected at the end of period 0; V_0 is the book value of capital employed at the end of period 0; V_1^* is the book value of capital employed at the end of period 1 which is expected at the end of period 0. Both book values are determined on the basis of the value-to-the-owner rules under the assumption that net realizable value never exceeds replacement cost. Hence equations 3.11 and 3.12 are used to establish actual and expected book values of capital employed. It should be noted that the ARR is defined in terms of net cash flows and initial and terminal book values of capital: in practice, of course, the net cash flows are unlikely to be known and the ARR will probably have to be deduced from ARPs and book values of capital in the manner discussed in Section 3.3.

The present value of the activity at the end of period 0 is given by

$$PV_0 = \frac{F_1^* - K_1^*}{1+\rho} + \frac{EV_1^*}{1+\rho} \tag{4.2}$$

where PV_0 is present value at the end of period 0, EV_1^* is the economic value of the activity at the end of period 1 which is expected at the end of period 0, and ρ is the cost of capital. Note that present value is defined in terms of the expected cash flows which occur at the end of period 1 and the expected economic value of the activity at the end of period 1. This allows for the possibility that at the end of period 1 the net realizable value of the activity exceeds its present value at that time: in such circumstances it is more profitable to end the activity at the end of period 1 rather than to continue it into subsequent periods, and hence the present value of the activity at the end of period 0 would be based on expected NRV at the end of period 1. Of course if expected PV at the end of period 1 exceeds expected NRV, then it is more profitable to continue the activity into period 2 than to end it, and then PV at the end of period 0 would be based on expected PV at the end of period 1.

We wish to show that if the expected ARR over period 1 exceeds the cost of capital then the activity should be undertaken at the start of period 1, while if the expected ARR is less than the cost of capital then the activity should not be undertaken at that time. To do this we must examine the implications for the relationship between present value, net realizable value, and replacement cost at the end of period 0 of different expected book values of capital at the end of period 1 and different relationships between the expected ARR and the cost of capital.

Subtracting equation 4.1 from 4.2 and rearranging, we find that

$$PV_0 - V_0 = \frac{EV_1^* - V_1^*}{1+\rho} + \frac{V_0(\alpha^* - \rho)}{1+\rho} \tag{4.3}$$

Equation 4.3, together with equations 3.11 and 3.12 which represent the value-to-the-owner rules when replacement cost is assumed to be never less than net realizable value, forms the cornerstone of our analysis.

We begin with the case where the expected ARR over period 1 exceeds the cost of capital, i.e. $\alpha^* > \rho$. We know from equation 3.12 that if book values of capital employed are determined on the basis of value-to-the-owner conventions, then economic value can never be less than book value: it follows that $EV_1^* - V_1^*$ in equation 4.3 must be non-negative. It is therefore clear from equation 4.3 that $\alpha^* > \rho$ implies that $PV_0 > V_0$, whatever the basis of expected book value at the end of period 1. From equation 3.11 we see that the present value of an activity exceeds its book value if and only if present value is greater than replacement cost, so we can conclude that $\alpha^* > \rho$ implies that $PV_0 > RC_0$. However this is not sufficient on its own to justify undertaking the activity at the end of period 0: even if $PV_0 > RC_0$ it is possible that PV_1^* exceeds RC_1^* by more, so making it worthwhile to defer undertaking the activity until the end of period 1. It is clear that deferral is not worthwhile if $V_1^* = EV_1^*$, for then

$RC_1^* \geqslant EV_1^*$ (from equation 3.12). Deferral can only be profitable when $EV_1^* > V_1^*$; in this case $PV_1^* > V_1^*$ and $V_1^* = RC_1^*$, but we can see from the second term on the right-hand side of equation 4.3 that when $\alpha^* > \rho$ PV_0 exceeds $RC_0(= V_0)$ by more than the value of the difference between PV_1^* and RC_1^* discounted at the cost of capital. Thus the value of undertaking the activity at the end of period 0 is greater than the value of waiting until the end of period 1: the returns accruing at the end of period 1 justify commencing the activity at the end of period 0.

Thus we see that an expected ARR over period 1 computed on the basis of the value-to-the-owner rules set out in equations 3.11 and 3.12 which exceeds the cost of capital unambiguously implies that the activity should be undertaken at the end of period 0. The analysis can be extended straightforwardly to the many-period case (as is done in the appendix to this chapter), so that the conclusion that an expected ARR in excess of the cost of capital is appropriately interpreted as a signal to undertake the activity is quite general.

We next consider the case where the expected ARR over period 1 is less than the cost of capital, i.e. $\alpha^* < \rho$. In these circumstances it follows from equation 4.3 that

$$PV_0 - V_0 < \frac{EV_1^* - V_1^*}{1 + \rho} \tag{4.4}$$

and hence a new activity should not be started at the end of period 0. This is obvious when $EV_1^* = V_1^*$, for then $PV_0 < V_0$ and we see from equation 3.11 that present value is less than book value if and only if $PV_0 < NRV_0$, so that not only is it not worthwhile to start a new activity but it is also profitable to stop undertaking an existing one. If $EV_1^* > V_1^*$ then it is not possible to conclude anything about the relationship between PV_0, RC_0 and NRV_0 from $\alpha^* < \rho$. But even if $PV_0 > RC_0$, $\alpha^* < \rho$ indicates that a new activity should not be started at the end of period 0: substituting PV_1^* for EV_1^* and RC_1^* for V_1^* in equation 4.4 we see that

$$PV_0 - RC_0 < \frac{PV_1^* - RC_1^*}{1 + \rho}$$

so that the expected excess of present value over replacement cost at the end of period 1 discounted at the cost of capital is greater than the excess of present value over replacement cost at the end of period 0, and hence it is profitable to defer starting the activity until the end of period 1. This is because the activity does not yield returns at the end of period 1 that compensate adequately for the opportunity cost of financing the activity at the end of period 0.

Thus an expected ARR over period 1 (computed on value-to-the-owner conventions) which is less than the cost of capital is an unambiguous indication that a new activity should not be undertaken at the end of period 0. However it is not clear, in such circumstances, whether or not an existing activity should be discontinued. As we have noted, if $EV_1^* = V_1^*$ then $\alpha^* < \rho$

indicates that termination of an existing activity is desirable, but if $EV_1^* > V_1^*$, $\alpha^* < \rho$ is quite compatible with $PV_0 > NRV_0$ in which case an existing activity should be continued. The ambiguity here can be resolved by calculating an expected ARR using net realizable value at the end of period 0 as the initial book value of capital: if this is less than the cost of capital the existing activity should unambiguously be terminated at the end of period 0, and possibly recommenced at the end of period 1 (if the expected ARR computed on value-to-the-owner conventions at the end of period 1 exceeds the cost of capital). These conclusions extend to the many-period case, as is shown in the appendix to this chapter.

Finally we consider the case where the expected ARR over period 1 equals the cost of capital, i.e. $\alpha^* = \rho$. Equation 4.3 now becomes

$$PV_0 - V_0 = \frac{EV_1^* - V_1^*}{1 + \rho} \tag{4.5}$$

If $EV_1^* = V_1^*$ then $\alpha^* = \rho$ implies that $PV_0 = V_0$, and from equation 3.11 we see that this implies that $NRV_0 \leqslant PV_0 \leqslant RC_0$. An existing activity should therefore be continued, but a new one should almost certainly not be started: at best the returns from starting a new activity at the end of period 0 just cover the costs of doing so. If $EV_1^* > V_1^*$ (so that $PV_1^* > RC_1^*$) then $PV_0 > V_0$ and hence $PV_0 > RC_0$. An existing activity should definitely be continued, while so far as a new activity is concerned it can be seen that the excess of present value over replacement cost at the end of period 0 is exactly equal to the expected excess of present value over replacement cost at the end of period 1 discounted at the cost of capital, so that starting a new activity at the end of period 0 is just as profitable as doing so at the end of period 1.

Thus when the expected ARR over period 1 (computed on value-to-the-owner conventions) equals the cost of capital, an existing activity should unambiguously be continued, while new activities should almost certainly not be started. The slight ambiguity in the conclusion for new activities arises because it is possible that an expected ARR over period 1 equal to the cost of capital indicates that the returns from starting a new activity at the end of period 0 just cover the cost of doing so. As in the other two cases these conclusions extend to the multi-period case.

To summarize the discussion in this section, we have seen that the comparison of the expected ARR over a segment of an activity's lifetime (computed using value-to-the-owner rules and assuming that replacement cost is never less than net realizable value) with the cost of capital provides a great deal of relevant information. If the expected ARR exceeds the cost of capital, starting a new activity is worthwhile, as is (*a fortiori*) the continuation of an existing one. If the expected ARR equals the cost of capital, then starting a new activity is almost certainly not worthwhile (although doing so may yield returns which just cover costs), but continuing an existing activity is worthwhile. If the expected ARR is less than the cost of capital then starting a new activity is not worthwhile, but the signal for existing activities is ambiguous, and needs to be clarified by computing an expected ARR in which terminal book value is determined on the basis of value-to-the-owner rules while initial book value is given by net realizable value.

4.3.   Valuing assets in the *ex ante* analysis

An application of the value-to-the-owner rules at the level of the individual asset therefore indicates whether an investment should be undertaken, not undertaken, or postponed, and whether an existing asset should be sold.

In many cases, however, we will be concerned with whether a group of assets should be purchased, whether a firm should expand its activities in general, or whether there should be entry into an industry. In that case we wish to evaluate investment in a set of assets. Application of the value-to-the-owner rules presents no special difficulties here because we are considering replication or disposal of a group of assets or a firm. If expansion is being considered then the cost of expansion will be the replacement cost of replicating the entire group of assets or the firm. If disposal is at issue then we are assessing the value that can be realized from selling the group of assets or ceasing the firm's operations. In both cases then the correct procedure is to apply the value-to-the-owner rules at the aggregate level of the group of assets and define the accounting value of the capital stock as

$$\min \left\{ \mathrm{RC}\left(\sum_j j \right), \max\left[\mathrm{PV}\left(\sum_j j \right), \mathrm{NRV}\left(\sum_j j \right) \right] \right\}. \qquad (4.6)$$

For the *ex ante* analysis, the replacement cost, present value, and net realizable value of the group of assets under consideration are evaluated and the value-to-the-owner rules are then applied to these aggregates as described in Section 3.4.

4.4   The use of the ARR in assessing performance

We now consider the use of the *ex post* accounting rate of return, calculated on the basis of value-to-the-owner conventions but using actual (out-turn) data, in assessing the performance of activities. As in Section 4.2 we use a simple one-period example to illustrate our arguments. At the end of period 1, *ex post* accounting data covering the period will be available. The analysis of *ex post* accounting data is not equivalent to *ex ante* analysis with correct information, because when expectations are not fulfilled, accountants do not go back to reassess previous valuations with the benefit of hindsight. Thus the *ex post* ARR is calculated using the book value which was attributed to capital employed at the end of period 0 on the basis of the expectations which were held at that time. Hence the *ex post* ARR computed using value-to-the-owner rules is given by

$$V_0 = \frac{F_1 - K_1}{1 + \alpha} + \frac{V_1}{1 + \alpha} \tag{4.7}$$

where, as in the previous section, the subscripts on α have been suppressed for simplicity. The absence of stars on F_1, K_1, and V_1 indicates that these are now actual rather than expected values, and V_0 and V_1 are determined according to equations 3.11 and 3.12.

The correct (i.e. with the benefit of hindsight) estimate of present value at the end of period 0 is $\overline{PV}_0$ where

$$\overline{PV}_0 = \frac{F_1 - K_1}{1 + \rho} + \frac{EV_1}{1 + \rho} \tag{4.8}$$

We define the difference between the actual estimate of present value which was made at the end of period 0 and the correct estimate as the error in present value expectations at the end of period 0, ε_0, so that

$$\overline{PV}_0 = PV_0 + \varepsilon_0. \tag{4.9}$$

As in the previous section we consider what can be inferred from a comparison of the *ex post* ARR using value-to-the-owner rules with the cost of capital. The results, although derived in a one-period example, all extend to the many-period case, as is shown in the appendix to this chapter. Subtracting equation 4.7 from 4.8 and rearranging gives the following equation, which is central to our analysis in this section:

$$\overline{PV}_0 - V_0 = \frac{EV_1 - V_1}{1 + \rho} + \frac{V_0(\alpha - \rho)}{1 + \rho}. \tag{4.10}$$

We begin with the case where the *ex post* ARR exceeds the cost of capital, i.e. $\alpha > \rho$. We know that under the value-to-the-owner rules, economic value can never be less than book value (see equation 3.12), so that $EV_1 - V_1$ is non-negative. Hence, from equation 4.10, if $\alpha > \rho$ then $\overline{PV}_0 > V_0$: the correct estimate of present value at the end of period 0 was greater than the book value of capital employed at that time. Substituting for $\overline{PV}_0$ from equation 4.9 we find that if $\alpha > \rho$, then

$$PV_0 + \varepsilon_0 > V_0$$

so that one of two possibilities must be true. Either $\varepsilon_0 > 0$, so that expectations were more than fulfilled during period 1, or $PV_0 > V_0$, which implies (from the value-to-the-owner rules expressed in equation 3.11) that $PV_0 > RC_0$. In this latter case, when the present value of a firm based on expectations held at the end of period 0 exceeds the replacement cost of its assets at that time, then it was certainly worthwhile to undertake the activity at the end of period 0. When the activity in question is a firm, a situation where present value based on expectations held at the end of period 0 exceeds replacement cost, where the latter is measured as the cost to a hypothetical competitor of creating a similar organization, provides evidence of barriers to entry sustaining monopoly power on the part of the firm. The qualifications which have to be borne in mind in practice when interpreting $PV_0 > RC_0$ as prima-facie evidence of monopoly power relate to the difficulties of measuring replacement cost correctly, as were discussed in Section 3.5, and these will be considered shortly.

We now consider the case where the *ex post* ARR is less than the cost of capital, i.e. $\alpha < \rho$. If the book value of capital at the end of period 1 equals economic value at the end of period 1 then we can see from equation 4.10 that $\alpha < \rho$ implies that $\overline{PV}_0 < V_0$. Substituting for $\overline{PV}_0$ in equation 4.9 we have

$$PV_0 + \varepsilon_0 < V_0$$

and so if $\alpha < \rho$, either $\varepsilon_0 < 0$ so that expectations were disappointed during period 1, or $PV_0 < V_0$, which (from equation 3.11) implies that $PV_0 < NRV_0$, and hence provides evidence that the continuation of the activity was not worthwhile at the end of period 0. Unfortunately matters are more complicated if economic value at the end of period 1 exceeds book value: in such circumstances it is clear from equation 4.10 that when $\alpha < \rho$, the relationship between PV_0 and V_0 is ambiguous, which means that it is not possible to deduce anything about the relationship of present value based on expectations held at the end of period 0 to either replacement cost or net realizable value at that time. Thus the overall conclusion is that it is necessary to know the basis on which the book value of capital employed at the end of period 1 is established before it is possible to infer anything from the *ex post* ARR being less than the cost of capital. If the terminal book value equals economic value then we can say that $\alpha < \rho$ implies either that expectations were disappointed or that the expected returns to the activity over the period did not justify its continued operation (which in the case of a firm provides prima-facie evidence of barriers to exit), but if terminal book value equals replacement cost nothing can be said.

Finally we consider the case where the *ex post* ARR equals the cost of capital, i.e. $\alpha = \rho$. From equation 4.10 we see that if $EV_1 = V_1$, $\alpha = \rho$ implies that $\overline{PV}_0 = V_0$. It is difficult to conclude anything very definite from this equality: expectations may have been exceeded or disappointed during the period, while present value based on expectations held at the end of period 0 may have been greater or less than book value at that time, so that it is not possible to say anything about its relationship to replacement cost or net realizable value at the end of period 0. However if $EV_1 > V_1$, then we see from equation 4.10 that $\alpha = \rho$ implies that $\overline{PV}_0 > V_0$, and the same argument as was used above in the case where $\alpha > \rho$ shows that this inequality implies that either expectations were exceeded during period 1, or $PV_0 > RC_0$, with the same implications for the assessment of the activity's performance.

Bringing these results together we see that if the *ex post* ARR exceeds the cost of capital, then this implies either that expectations were more than fulfilled during the period in question, or that present value at the start of the period, based on expectations held at that time, exceeded replacement cost. Therefore it was certainly worthwhile to undertake the activity, and, if possible, the activity should have been expanded. The interpretation of the situation where the *ex post* ARR is less than or equal to the cost of capital is more complicated, and it is necessary to know the relationship of the book value of capital employed at the end of the period to economic value and replacement cost before anything definite can be said about these cases. The appendix to this chapter shows that these results all generalize to the many-period case.

The result concerning the interpretation of the *ex post* ARR computed on value-to-the-owner conventions exceeding the cost of capital is one of great value in attempting to assess the performance of activities. An application which is of particular interest to economists and regulators involves the use of ARRs in excess of the cost of capital as indicators of monopoly power. As has been noted, however, there are a number of practical difficulties in using the above theoretical results in this way. It is far from straightforward to measure the cost to a hypothetical competitor of creating a similar organization, which is the correct concept of replacement cost for a firm as a whole, because of the need to include in this measure the cost of intangibles such as goodwill, advertising, research and development, and so on, and to distinguish how much expenditure on these would be actually necessary to create a similar organization as opposed to creating barriers to entry. So it must be realized that an ARR above the cost of capital, even when it is known that expectations have been fulfilled, is not in practice an unambiguous sign of monopoly power (nor for that matter is an ARR equal to the cost of capital a definite signal of the absence of monopoly power). Detailed investigations will still be required to supplement the evidence provided by ARRs before competition policy is brought to bear on a firm. But it must also be realized that the estimation of the replacement cost of a firm by accountants, though inevitably subject to a high degree of uncertainty, is likely to be as good an estimate as can be hoped for, and hence it is not unreasonable to regard an *ex post* ARR in excess of the cost of capital as a prima-facie indication of monopoly power if it is known that expectations have been fulfilled.

Another difficulty in the practical application of these results, which is relevant for all uses of the *ex post* ARR, is of course to distinguish cases of unfulfilled expectations from those where expected returns did or did not justify the operation of the activity. We discuss this problem in the context of identifying potential monopoly power, but the general principles apply to all uses of the *ex post* ARR. The test that must be applied by any investigator is that of persistence. An *ex post* ARR which is calculated for each of a number of successive years and is persistently above the cost of capital suggests that the high ARR is a prima-facie indicator of monopoly power, as systematic over-fulfilment of expectations over a number of years is rather implausible. An investigator will often be assisted in trying to distinguish unfulfilled expectations from potential barriers to entry as explanations of high *ex post* ARRs by the existence of alternative data sources. If actual (*ex ante*) present values (PV_0 in the notation above) are observable, then a comparison with the *ex post* present value based on hindsight ($\overline{PV_0}$) immediately provides evidence of incorrect expectations. The stock market value of a company's shares does provide a market assessment of the present value of expected returns to shareholders, and so can be used for the purpose of identifying mistaken expectations. Stock market data can be used to analyse *ex post* whether the return on a company's shares was above or below the return on the market as a whole (appropriately adjusted for risk): if the return is above that of the market as a whole, then this is evidence of performance having exceeded expectations, and conversely if the company return is less than that of the market. It should be noted that studies which employ market valuations in analyses of rates of return are no more and no less than assessments of unfulfilled expectations. They can provide no evidence on whether or not rates of return on invested assets exceeded the cost of capital, because, if assets are valued at the present value of the expected future net cash flows to which they give rise discounted at the cost of capital, then the rate of return on those assets will equal the cost of capital if expectations are fulfilled and differ from it if expectations are not fulfilled. The *ex post* analysis of stock market rates of return does, however, provide just the information that is required to identify whether or not expectations were fulfilled over a period. The conclusion we reach is thus that a combination of *ex post* analyses of the ARR (using the value-to-the-owner rules) and the stock market rate of return is relevant in attempting to assess whether firms possess monopoly power.

One final problem concerning the use of the *ex post* ARR to assess performance needs to be mentioned, and this arises when the *ex post* ARR equals the cost of capital. As we have seen, if the terminal book value of capital employed equals economic value it is difficult to conclude anything definite from the equality of the *ex post* ARR and the cost of capital. But suppose that terminal book value was equal to economic value and we were sure that expectations had been fulfilled over the period for which the *ex post* ARR was measured: then $\alpha = \rho$ would imply that $PV_0 = V_0$; the initial book value of capital employed was equal to present value. Under the value-to-the-owner rules, this situation arises when $RC_0 \geqslant PV_0 \geqslant NRV_0$ (see equation 3.11 above). It is clear that if there is a significant difference between replacement cost and net realizable value the equality of the *ex post* ARR and the cost of capital can conceal substantial variations in the performance of an activity: for example a firm with PV_0 fractionally below RC_0 would have an *ex post* ARR equal to the cost of capital (if expectations were fulfilled) as would another firm with PV_0 only just above NRV_0, but the performance of these two firms is clearly rather different, with the first being virtually in a sustainable long-run position while the returns to the second are only just sufficient to avoid immediate liquidation.

4.5   Valuing assets in the *ex post* analysis

The valuation of assets in the *ex ante* analysis was seen to be conceptually straightforward: value all component assets at one of replacement cost, present value, or net realizable value. Valuation in the *ex post* case is somewhat different because here we are concerned with a rather different set of questions. We are now looking back and saying how well a single project or group of projects has actually performed. As far as possible we then wish to attribute this performance to one of three possible explanations: luck (mistaken expectations), skill (superior management), and inherent advantages (barriers to entry).

We have already considered mistaken expectations and concluded that persistence is the best way in practice of establishing systematic factors. The rest of the discussion will therefore abstract from the problem of determining whether expectations were fulfilled. Evidence for superior performance in one of the other two senses comes from a present value of net earnings in excess of the cost of replicating the activity of a firm. If the firm is earning a net revenue stream whose present value (over the relevant period being examined) is greater than the cost of replicating the firm's assets, then the only explanation for why others have not actually replicated is that they do not possess either the ability or the opportunity. Likewise if the firm is earning a return below that required to produce a normal return on its disposal value, then it is either being badly managed or constrained in the actions that it can pursue.

But notice what is involved in the act of replication as against investment. If a firm comprises a number of assets (whose costs and values are determined on the basis described previously) then it is likely that for some of the component assets economic value at the beginning and end of the period is in excess of replacement cost and for some economic value is below replacement cost. For the former the firm, if deprived of these assets, would choose to replace them; for the latter it would not. Replication at minimum cost therefore involves replacing the former assets at replacement cost and the latter at economic value. In the *ex post* analysis, replacement cost is thus defined as,

$$\sum_{i=1}^{N} \min(RC_i, EV_i) \tag{4.11}$$

(provided $EV_i \geqslant RC_i$ for at least one i) where the firm is assumed to possess N assets $i = 1 \ldots N$. But the replacement cost of the firm as a whole may be less than this summation of the replacement cost of the individual assets so that the aggregate replacement cost has to be defined as,

$$\min\left\{ \sum_{i=1}^{N} \min(RC_i, EV_i), RC \right\} \tag{4.12}$$

where RC is the cost of replacing the total of the firm's assets.

The difference between aggregation across assets in the *ex ante* and *ex post* analyses comes from the fact that in the former, the firm is by definition purchasing new assets. In the latter, however, the replication of the firm may involve the employment of assets that are currently under the possession of the firm. An outside replacement cost is thus not relevant to a replication decision in this particular case.

Having defined exact replication we are now in a position to establish the cause of excess returns. We relax the assumption of exact replication by assuming either that any management other than the present management has access to the firm's resources, or that the existing management only has access to the opportunities available to outside firms. If excess returns persist in the former case then they are at least in part attributable to barriers to entry. If they persist in the latter case then they are at least in part attributable to superior management.

The replacement cost of a new firm attempting to replicate the activities of an existing firm will differ on a number of counts. First, there may be economies or diseconomies of scale or scope associated with the combination of the activities in question with existing assets. Recall from Section 3.5 that the replacement cost of a particular asset is established as the replacement cost of the firm as a whole less the replacement cost of the firm excluding this asset. The relationship between the stand-alone replacement cost and that incurred by a firm is dependent on how new assets can be integrated with existing ones. Secondly, the firm whose assets are being replicated may have access to resources on superior terms. It may receive preferential contracts that confer economic advantages on the firm. More interestingly, we have noted above that some component assets may have an economic value below replacement cost. If we value these at the cost of replacing them as against their economic value then the capital cost of entry will be correspondingly higher. Thus a competitor faces a cost disadvantage in replicating an existing firm in so far as it would not choose to acquire some of the assets that are already in the possession of the existing firm. These assets will be maintained in operation but would not be replaced were the firm to be deprived of them. If these three cost disadvantages of a potential rival (economies of scale or scope, cost advantages, or assets in place) are sufficient to explain a decision not to enter then the abnormal return of the existing firm can be attributed to a barrier to entry.

However, if the existing firm's replacement costs are equal to those of a potential rival (i.e. all assets are valued at replacement costs not economic value and outside firms can attain similar replacement costs for component assets) then the abnormal return of the existing firm must be attributable to superior management. This follows since we are saying that even if the firm has access to resources on the same terms as outside firms then it still can earn an abnormal return. The ability of a management to earn excess returns on an opportunity open to others must be evidence of superior skill.

We can illustrate this in relation to the most important class of assets for which replacement cost is in excess of economic value—goodwill. If goodwill reflects the past investments that a firm has made in building up a reputation then it may be close to impossible for a new firm to attempt to replicate instantaneously the reputation of the existing firm. Reputations can by definition only be acquired over time so that it will often be the case that the replacement cost of this type of goodwill will be well in excess of its economic value. If we wish to compute replacement cost assuming exact replication then we would include goodwill at economic value. The return earned on the firm's goodwill is a normal one unless during the period in question the firm built on its reputation and increased its economic value over and above that which was anticipated at the start. From the point of view of measuring the performance of the firm this is entirely appropriate. The minimum cost at which the assets of the firm could be replicated is either the cost of purchasing from outside, or in the case of the goodwill, its economic value at the start of the period. But from the point of view of a firm contemplating entering the market, the cost of attempting to replicate its goodwill will be well in excess of its economic value. Thus exact replication will not be attempted and subsequent excess returns may be attributable to this competitive advantage.

But notice that one of the primary objectives of the analysis is to associate abnormal returns with specific time periods and actions. Quite rightly the firm only earns a normal return if actions taken after the opening period do not further augment the goodwill of the firm. To put this another way the opening and closing valuations and the costs should discount the value of actions taken up to the two periods. If a firm has gained a strong reputation in the past, then that is included in its economic valuation, and the replacement cost of this is the present value of the cost of replicating this reputation at the opening period. Subsequently actions will be taken that will augment or diminish this valuation and these are appropriately attributed to the time period under study. Thus to return to the example of goodwill described above, if we want to determine the contribution of management decisions taken to performance between T_1 and T_2 then we should value the goodwill in relation to decisions taken to T_1 (assuming that decisions are taken that yield normal returns thereafter) and then value the goodwill in relation to decisions taken to T_2. Only if decisions taken between T_1 and T_2 augment economic value over and above a normal return will management performance between T_1 and T_2 have been abnormal.

We thus emerge with some precise criteria on which to establish valuation. If the principles described in equations 4.11 and 4.12 are followed, the abnormal returns are either due to good management or opportunities that were not open to others. We can establish which is the contributory factor by undertaking valuations of assets on the basis of opportunities open to competitors. If when valuing assets on the basis of opportunities available to competitors, abnormal returns persist, then superior managerial performance is suggested. Furthermore we can attribute managerial performance to particular time periods by valuing assets on the basis of actions taken to the opening and closing periods.

Consider, for example, the question considered in Chapter 3 as to whether the expenditures made by a firm on a research and development programme should be capitalized or treated as a current expenditure. The above discussion suggests that the value of the activities undertaken to periods T_1 and T_2 should be recorded as opening and closing valuations if less than the current cost of replicating these activities. Otherwise replacement costs should be used. Then abnormal returns will be earned between T_1 and T_2 if actions taken between these two periods alter the probability of successful outcomes and the returns associated with these outcomes.

4.6 Conclusion

The analysis of this chapter has shown that if book values of capital employed are determined on the basis of value-to-the-owner conventions, and all changes in book values flow through the profit and loss account, then the accounting rate of return over a segment (of whatever size) of an activity's lifetime provides information which, in a great many cases, is directly relevant for economists, investors, regulators, and others who are concerned to assess the performance of activities. Contrary to what is often supposed, therefore, appropriately defined accounting profitability measures can be extremely useful for economic analysis. Our arguments in this chapter provide theoretical support for an accounting valuation convention which has been widely adopted in the past decade during the course of the debate on inflation accounting, but which has usually been regarded as a pragmatic compromise between competing pure valuation bases with little theoretical justification. The justification we offer is that the ARR which is computed from accounting profitability measures based on value-to-the-owner conventions can in many cases (sometimes in conjunction with additional information) be given a straightforward economic interpretation. In fact the annual accounting rate of profit given by value-to-the-owner conventions and fully articulated accounts is the ARR for a one-year segment of an activity's life, and there is much to be said for using this ARR for economic analysis. Not only does it avoid the need for iterative calculations based on equation 3.10 above, it also provides a large number of ARRs over time so facilitating the persistence test required to distinguish expected from unexpectedly good or bad performance when *ex post* ARRs are being used. Table 4.1 summarizes the results that we have derived in this chapter.

Our analysis in this chapter does not mean that economists should make uncritical use of accounting profitability data. First, we have noted in Sections 4.3 and 4.5 that care is required in applying the value-to-the-owner rules at the aggregate level of a group of assets, firm or industry. The

Table 4.1. Accounting rate of return signals

Summary of ex ante Results
($\alpha^* = ex\ ante$ ARR; $\rho = $ Cost of capital)

$\alpha^* > \rho$ New activity should be undertaken at beginning of period

$\alpha^* = \rho$ New activity should not commence. Existing activities should continue

$\alpha^* < \rho$ New activity should not be undertaken at beginning of period. Existing activity should cease if initial accounting valuation is on net realizable basis (with possible recommencement at a later date)

Summary of ex post Results
($\alpha = ex\ post$ ARR; $\rho = $ Cost of capital)

$\alpha > \rho$ Expectations were more than fulfilled or prima-facie evidence of a barrier to entry

$\alpha < \rho$ If closing book value of capital is economic value, then either expectations were disappointed or prima-facie evidence of a barrier to exit

---

procedures that are required to aggregate for the *ex ante* and *ex post* analyses are different: in the former the rules should be applied at the aggregate level of the group of assets and in the latter in certain cases they should be applied at the level of the individual asset. Secondly, care is required in interpreting rankings of ARRs. We noted that in the single period case where $\alpha^* > \rho$, the acceleration of a project from the end to the beginning of the period may be signalled. Likewise, in those cases in which terminal book value is measured at replacement cost, the ranking of activities with $\alpha^* > \rho$ reflects the relative desirability of *accelerating* implementation.[2] A third reason for caution in the use of accounting profitability figures computed on the basis of value to the owner is the inevitable uncertainty involved in estimating the current values of the activities in question which form the basis of the value-to-the-owner rules, especially when these are calculated for a concern as a whole. Finally, although the value-to-the-owner rules have received widespread support from accounting bodies throughout the world over the past decade, historic cost valuation conventions were dominant previously, and still exert enormous influence on accounting practice. We would not derive the results of this chapter for book values based on historic cost, and the use of historic cost profitability figures for economic analysis cannot be justified within our framework. But this means that our analysis has important implications for accounting criteria themselves: it provides a basis on which accountants can discriminate between the alternative rules and standards available to them by reference to their relevance to the information required by investors and regulators. We pursue this theme in the following chapters which consider two controversial areas in accounting—inflation accounting and the appropriate treatment of deferred taxation.

Notes

1. For example Fama (1972) discusses the conditions under which the Capital Asset Pricing Model is applicable in a multiperiod context.
2. This can be seen as follows. Assuming perfect certainty, as the point at issue does not depend on the existence of uncertainty, and dividing equation 4.3 by V_0, we have

$$\frac{PV_0 - V_0}{V_0} = \frac{EV_1 - V_1}{V_0(1 + \rho)} + \frac{\alpha - \rho}{1 + \rho}$$

If $\alpha > \rho$ and $EV_1 \geqslant RC_1$ then this equation can be written as

$$\frac{PV_0 - RC_0}{RC_0} - \frac{PV_1 - RC_1}{RC_0(1 + \rho)} = \frac{\alpha - \rho}{1 + \rho}$$

in which case rankings of α relate to benefits of accelerating implementation.

Appendix

In this appendix a number of results which were derived using a very simple example in Sections 4.2 and 4.4 of Chapter 4 are shown to hold much more generally. Using a continuous time framework, the analysis in this appendix shows that all the results discussed in the main text extend to the many-period case.

We begin with some definitions. Let $F(t)$ denote the revenue generated at t, $K(t)$ the new capital required at t, $V(t)$ the book value of capital employed at t, and ρ the instantaneous cost of capital (which is taken to be constant for simplicity). We consider a segment in the life of a continuing activity, extending from time T_1 to time T_2. We start with the problem of evaluating returns during the segment (T_1, T_2) from the viewpoint of expectations held at T_1, which are assumed to be single-valued and held with certainty: this corresponds to the analysis in Section 4.2 of the main text.

The present value of the activity at T_1 is

$$PV(T_1) = \int_{T_1}^{T_2} (F^*(t) - K^*(t))e^{-\rho(t - T_1)}\, dt + e^{-\rho(T_2 - T_1)}EV^*(T_2) \quad \text{(A4.1)}$$

where an asterisk indicates the value of a variable which is expected at time T_1 and

$$EV(t) = \max(PV(t), NRV(t)) \quad \text{(A4.2)}$$

denotes the economic value of an activity at t, which is the maximum of its present value at t ($PV(t)$) or its net realizable value at t ($NRV(t)$).

The expected accounting rate of return (ARR) of the activity over the segment (T_1, T_2), computed using value-to-the-owner rules for the book value of capital employed, is defined by α^* such that

$$V(T_1) = \int_{T_1}^{T_2} (F^*(t) - K^*(t))e^{-\alpha^*(t-T_1)}\, dt + e^{-\alpha^*(T_2 - T_1)}V^*(T_2) \quad \text{(A4.3)}$$

where

$$V(t) = \min(\text{RC}(t),\ \text{EV}(t)) \quad \text{(A4.4)}$$

where $\text{RC}(t)$ denotes the replacement cost of the activity at t. We make the important assumption throughout the analysis that

$$\text{RC}(t) \geqslant \text{NRV}(t)\ \forall\, t. \quad \text{(A4.5)}$$

The justification for this assumption is discussed in the main text.

First consider the case where $V(T_2) = \text{EV}(T_2)$. Then, from equations A4.1 and A4.3, we have that

$$\alpha^* \gtreqqless \rho \text{ as } V(T_1) \lesseqqgtr \text{PV}(T_1)$$

and hence, using equations A4.2, A4.4, and A4.5

$$\alpha^* \gtreqqless \rho \text{ as } V(T_1) \begin{cases} = \text{RC}(T_1) < \text{PV}(T_1) \\ = \text{PV}(T_1) \\ = \text{NRV}(T_1) > \text{PV}(T_1). \end{cases} \quad \text{(A4.6)}$$

Equation A4.6 shows that when $V^*(T_2) = \text{EV}^*(T_2)$, decisions as to whether a new activity should be undertaken or an existing activity should be discontinued can be correctly made by comparing the forecast ARR computed using value-to-the-owner rules with the cost of capital.

Now consider the case where $\text{EV}^*(T_2) > V^*(T_2)$, so that $V^*(T_2) = \text{RC}^*(T_2)$. Subtracting equation A4.3 from A4.1 we have that

$$\alpha^* \gtreqqless \rho \text{ as } \text{PV}(T_1) - V(T_1) \gtreqqless (\text{PV}^*(T_2) - \text{RC}^*(T_2))e^{-\rho(T_2 - T_1)}. \quad \text{(A4.7)}$$

Using equation A4.4 and the fact that the right-hand side of equation A4.7 is positive by assumption gives

$$\alpha^* \geqq \rho \text{ as } \text{PV}(T_1) - \text{RC}(T_1) \geqq (\text{PV}^*(T_2) - \text{RC}^*(T_2))e^{-\rho(T_2 - T_1)} \quad \text{(A4.8)}$$

so that an expected ARR in excess of the cost of capital unambiguously indicates that an activity should be undertaken. If $\alpha^* < \rho$ then, from equation A4.7, one of the following three conditions must hold depending on the basis of the book value of capital at T_1:

$$V(T_1) = \text{RC}(T_1): \text{PV}(T_1) - \text{RC}(T_1) < (\text{PV}^*(T_2) - \text{RC}^*(T_2))e^{-\rho(T_2 - T_1)} \quad \text{(A4.9)}$$

$$V(T_1) = \text{PV}(T_1): 0 < (\text{PV}^*(T_2) - \text{RC}^*(T_2))e^{-\rho(T_2 - T_1)} \quad \text{(A4.10)}$$

$$V(T_1) = NRV(T_1): \quad PV(T_1) < NRV(T_1) + (PV^*(T_2) - RC^*(T_2))e^{-\rho(T_2-T_1)}$$
$$\text{(A4.11)}$$

It is clear from these three conditions that if $\alpha^* < \rho$, a new activity should not be undertaken at T_1, even if $PV^*(T_2) > RC^*(T_2)$. But the signal for an existing activity when $PV^*(T_2) > RC^*(T_2)$ and $\alpha^* < \rho$ is ambiguous: only if equation A4.11 holds should the activity be terminated at T_1 and possibly resumed at T_2.

Drawing equations A4.6, A4.8, and A4.9–11 together, it is clear that the results discussed in Section 4.2 of the main text continue to hold in the many-period context.

We now turn to the issue of evaluating the performance of activities *ex post*, using actual accounting data. This corresponds to Section 4.4 of Chapter 4. The *ex post* ARR over the segment (T_1, T_2) is defined by α such that

$$V(T_1) = \int_{T_1}^{T_2} (F(t) - K(t))e^{-\alpha(t-T_1)} \, dt + e^{-\alpha(T_2-T_1)}V(T_2). \quad \text{(A4.12)}$$

The correct (i.e. with the benefit of hindsight) estimate of the present value of the activity at T_1 is

$$\overline{PV}(T_1) = \int_{T_1}^{T_2} (F(t) - K(t))e^{-\rho(t-T_1)} \, dt + e^{-\rho(T_2-T_1)}EV(T_2). \quad \text{(A4.13)}$$

The error in present value expectations at T_1 is defined as $\varepsilon(T_1)$ such that

$$\overline{PV}(T_1) = PV(T_1) + \varepsilon(T_1). \quad \text{(A4.14)}$$

First, suppose that $EV(T_2) = V(T_2)$. Then from equations A4.12 and A4.13

$$\alpha \gtreqless \rho \text{ as } V(T_1) \lesseqgtr \overline{PV}(T_1). \quad \text{(A4.15)}$$

Using equations A4.2, A4.4, A4.5, and A4.14 it follows that:

(i) if $\alpha > \rho$, then either $PV(T_1) > RC(T_1)$, so that expansion of the activity was desirable at T_1, or $\varepsilon(T_1) > 0$, so that expectations were more than fulfilled during (T_1, T_2),

(ii) if $\alpha < \rho$, then either $NRV(T_1) > PV(T_1)$, so that contraction of the activity was desirable at T_1, or $\varepsilon(T_1) < 0$, so that expectations were disappointed during (T_1, T_2).

Now suppose that $EV(T_2) > V(T_2)$ so that $V(T_2) = RC(T_2)$. Using equations A4.12 and A4.13 we have

$$\alpha \gtreqless \rho \text{ as } \overline{PV}(T_1) - V(T_1) \gtreqless (PV(T_2') - RC(T_2))e^{-\rho(T_2-T_1)}. \quad \text{(A4.16)}$$

Thus $\alpha > \rho$ implies that $\overline{PV}(T_1) > RC(T_1)$ by more than the discounted excess of $PV(T_2)$ over $RC(T_2)$, and hence either $PV(T_1)$ exceeded $RC(T_1)$ by enough to justify expansion of the activity at T_1 or $\varepsilon(T_1) > 0$, so that expectations were more than fulfilled. However there is no obvious interpretation of $\alpha \leqslant \rho$ in this case.

Drawing equations A4.15 and A4.16 together again confirms that the results discussed in Section 4.4 of the main text continue to hold in the many-period framework.

5

Inflation Accounting I
The Case for Real Terms Accounts

5.1 Introduction

THE analysis of the previous chapter showed that accounting profitability data would be directly relevant for economic analysis, providing investors and regulators with appropriate signals about the performance of activities, if two basic principles were adhered to in the construction of the accounting data, and one rather weak assumption is made. The assumption is that the replacement cost (RC) of an asset should not be less than its net realizable value (NRV). While there is nothing in logic to rule out the possibility that the net realizable value of an asset exceeds its replacement cost, such a situation is unlikely to persist for long, for if NRV is greater than RC, firms will be able to make a sure profit by selling the assets they possess and buying new ones, and the resulting price changes will soon ensure that $RC \geqslant NRV$. The two basic principles which must apply in constructing the accounting data are, first, that capital employed should be valued using the value-to-the-owner rules, according to which book value is given by the minimum of replacement cost and the maximum of present value and net realizable value, and, second, that the accounts should be fully articulated, with the whole of any change over time in the book value of capital employed flowing through the profit and loss account during the intervening period.

As we saw in Chapter 3, the value-to-the-owner rules for the valuation of capital employed have become a common feature of inflation accounting standards in the English-speaking world over the past decade (sometimes in a modified form in which 'recoverable amount' is substituted for present value: see Tweedie and Whittington (1984) chapter 10 pp. 248–51). However, accountants are traditionally reluctant to recognize gains on holding assets as profits until they are realized, so that the second of our basic principles for the construction of accounting profitability data is far less widely accepted than is the first. Nevertheless, the view that accounting profits should include all gains on holding assets, whether realized or unrealized, has a distinguished pedigree in the academic accounting literature. Sweeney (1936) divided the profit and loss account into realized and unrealized sections, but showed at the bottom of the profit and loss statement the total of realized and unrealized income, which he called 'final net income for the period'. Edwards and Bell (1961) proposed a measure of 'realized profit' which included realized holding gains and a measure of 'business profit' which included unrealized holding gains as well. In arguing for this second basic principle to be employed in the construction of accounting profitability data, we do not wish to suggest that the division of holding gains into realized and unrealized gains may not provide much useful information for the users of accounts. However, the accounting measure of profit must include *all* changes in the value of capital employed, whatever their source, if the resulting accounting profitability figures are to be useful for economic analysis.

The purpose of the present chapter is to consider the issues involved in inflation accounting in the light of the principles which have emerged from the preceding theoretical discussion. In particular we wish to argue in favour of the Real Terms approach to inflation accounting, which combines current values for assets with general index adjustment of capital for the effects of inflation.

5.2   The measurement of inflation-adjusted profitability

Perhaps the first point to make in discussing inflation-adjusted accounting profitability measures is that it is not obvious that such adjustments are absolutely necessary. If an accounting rate of return is to be constructed from accounting profitability data for comparison with a measure of the cost of capital in order to judge the performance of an activity, then a case can be made for this accounting rate of return to be in nominal terms. The reason is simply that the measure of the cost of capital will usually be based on market interest rates and security yields, and these are generally in nominal terms, so that comparison with the accounting rate of return will be much simpler if the latter is also in nominal terms. In this case no inflation adjustments are required: at any date assets are valued according to the value-to-the-owner rules in terms of the prices appropriate to that date, and cash inflows and outflows are also measured in current price terms. Of course, if the accounting rate of return is to be interpreted in the manner discussed in the previous chapter then it is necessary for all changes in the book value of capital employed between any two periods to flow through the profit and loss account, and this implies that increases in the book value of capital due to a general rise in prices must be reflected in the depreciation charge. We require the following relationship between accounting profit in period t, Y_t, revenue generated in t, F_t, new capital required in t, K_t, and book value of capital employed at the end of period $t-1$, V_{t-1}, and period t, V_t, to hold:

$$Y_t = F_t - K_t + V_t - V_{t-1}. \tag{5.1}$$

Depreciation, D_t, is defined by

$$Y_t = F_t - D_t \tag{5.2}$$

and therefore must satisfy the following equation:

$$D_t = K_t + V_{t-1} - V_t. \tag{5.3}$$

If all variables are measured in current prices, it is clear from equation 5.3 that increases in the book value of capital employed due to a rise in the general price level must reduce the depreciation charge and hence boost accounting profits in period t in order for the resulting nominal accounting rate of return to be compared meaningfully with a nominal measure of the cost of capital.

The introduction to this book and the previous two chapters have emphasized that a profit concept is best described in relation to alternative opportunities—investment, disinvestment, entry, exit—or alternative scenarios —replacement of a management, changing the set of investments open to a firm. Associated with each of these alternative opportunities or scenarios is a book value of capital which yields a particular earnings figure. If these earnings are in nominal terms, then a comparison with the nominal earnings of the investment, firm or industry in question provides appropriate answers to the issues considered above. This comparison is summarized in the relation of nominal accounting rates of return to nominal costs of capital. The value-to-the-owner rules therefore serve to emphasize that inflation adjustments are irrelevant to a broad range of economically interesting questions. Once the appropriate opportunity cost of capital can be identified then provided that all assets are valued at current prices, be they at net realizable value, present value, or replacement cost, problems associated with identifying price indices for inflation adjustments do not arise.

Where they are of concern, however, is in trying to answer the other set of questions discussed in the introduction, namely those associated with distribution. If profit is to be used to determine the income accruing to shareholders in the Hicksian sense of feasible consumption while maintaining capital intact, then the real earnings potential of capital has to be established. For this purpose a price index to revalue closing capital measures in terms of opening ones is required.

There are two central concepts of capital maintenance: the proprietary approach and the entity approach.[1] The former views the firm's capital as a fund of wealth attributable to the proprietors—the equity shareholders. If the general price level is constant then it is the money value of opening capital which must be maintained before a profit is recognized. However, if the general price level changes, the real purchasing power of capital must be maintained, and this is derived by applying a general price index to yield a measure of capital which maintains its command over goods and services in general. In contrast the entity approach aims to preserve intact the operating capacity of the business—its ability to provide goods and services. This also leads to money capital maintenance if all prices are constant, but if there are relative price changes it requires opening money capital to be adjusted by changes in the prices of specific assets of the firm, so that the cost of maintaining the assets necessary to preserve productive capacity is deducted from revenue before a profit is recognized.

If accounting profitability data are to be useful for economic analysis, enabling assessments of the performance of activities to be made, then it seems clear that the appropriate concept of capital to be maintained is the proprietary one. The general approach that we have adopted in our discussion of accounting profitability data is to ask whether it provides information which enables one to assess how worthwhile a particular use of capital is. In particular, we want to be able to use these data in order to determine whether the present operating capacity of a firm *should* be maintained, rather than being committed to the maintenance of the existing form of a business as under the entity approach to capital maintenance. If accounting profitability data are to provide information enabling investors to make decisions about the allocation of their wealth between different uses then it is necessary to regard each individual firm as a stock of resources to be applied in whatever use is of most benefit to the shareholders. This means that the appropriate concept of capital to be maintained is a fund of general purchasing power which, under inflationary conditions, is adjusted by a general price index. It is difficult to see how efficient allocation decisions can be made on the basis of accounting profitability data if the latter are based on a concept of capital maintenance which regards each individual firm as a going concern that must preserve, at all costs, its ability to continue producing its goods and services.

We regard the above argument as being sufficient on its own for the use of a proprietary concept of capital maintenance rather than an entity one, but it is worth noting two others. One is that it is very difficult indeed to provide a measure of operating capacity as the basis of an entity capital maintenance concept. After an extensive discussion of the issues involved in defining operating capacity, Tweedie and Whittington (1984) state that 'it is tempting to conclude that the concept of operating capacity should be abandoned entirely' because of the complications involved in trying to measure it. In contrast, the proprietary concept of capital is relatively simple and objective. The other argument against the use of an entity capital maintenance concept is that because it is designed to compensate for changes in the prices of the specific assets of the firm holding gains on assets are never recognized as part of profit. As we have constantly emphasized, a basic principle which must apply in the construction of accounting profitability data if it is to be directly relevant for economic analysis is that all changes in the book value of capital employed must flow through the profit and loss account. A concept of capital maintenance which excludes increases in the current value of assets owned by the firm from profit obviously fails to satisfy this basic principle, and hence the entity concept of capital must be rejected.

Our rejection of the entity concept of capital maintenance means that we also reject the use of specific price indices in adjusting the value of capital which has to be maintained before a profit is recognized. It is clear that an index of the prices of the specific assets used by the firm will not be an appropriate index with which to measure whether the proprietors' interest has been maintained in terms of command over a basket of goods representative of that purchased by the average shareholder. The use of a general price index to adjust the value of the capital which is to be maintained will result in constant real capital representing approximately constant command over goods and services in the economy. It has to be recognized that a perfect price index does not exist, for shareholders will have differing tastes and consumption patterns and it is impossible for any one price index to ensure that constant real capital maintains a constant command over goods and services consumed by all shareholders. The important point is that some general index should be used in order to take account of changes in the general purchasing power of the monetary unit. Economists generally advocate the use of a consumer price index on the grounds that what matters to shareholders is the amount of real consumption a company affords them, not the quantities of goods a company buys or sells, except in so far as the latter are a means to that end. However, given that no perfect price index exists, it is also possible to make a case for using other general price indices. The essential point to note is that a general price index must be used to express capital and profit in terms of constant purchasing power.

To summarize the discussion in this section, our theoretical analysis suggests that the appropriate way in which to take account of inflation in the construction of accounting profitability data which will be relevant for economic analysis is to combine a current valuation base for capital employed—the value-to-the-owner rules—with general index adjustment of capital for the effects of inflation. The appropriate way to measure inflation-adjusted profit then emerges naturally from the requirement that all changes in the book value of capital employed should flow through the profit and loss account. This approach to inflation accounting, in which general index adjustment is superimposed on a current valuation basis, is known as Real Terms accounting and it has a distinguished intellectual history, which we consider in the next section, together with what we believe to be the advantages of our particular version of it.

5.3 Real Terms accounting

The Real Terms (RT) approach to inflation accounting can be traced back to the work of Sweeney (1936), who argued in favour of adjusting capital by a general price index for profit measurement purposes while valuing real assets at replacement cost. Sweeney distinguished between realized and unrealized gains in his treatment of appreciation, although proposing that both should be included in 'final net income'. Edwards and Bell (1961) also advocated the use of replacement cost values together with a general index adjustment of capital, but they proposed a far more detailed presentation of the profit and loss statement, in which a distinction was made between operating and holding gains, money gains and real gains, and realized and unrealized gains. Edwards and Bell's final measure of 'business profit' included all these items, but their approach provides a broad set of information about the effects of general and specific price changes. Chambers (1966) also proposed a RT approach, but in his view, general price index adjustment of capital was appropriately combined with net realizable value as the current valuation base. In contrast, Baxter (1975) suggested value to the owner as the appropriate current value base of a RT system, although he excluded unrealized gains from the definition of profit, reporting them only in the shareholders' equity interest in the balance sheet. An adaptation of the value-to-the-owner base has also been proposed by Edwards and Bell in their more recent work (Edwards, Bell and Johnson (1979)). They advocate a mixture of 'entry values' (replacement cost) and 'exit values' (net realizable value) together with general index adjustment of capital and a number of distinctions between the component parts of 'business profit' as in their earlier work.

It is clear from this summary of the history of RT accounting proposals that the general approach is not new, and the version of it that we support, with the current valuation base being value to the owner, and all changes in the value of capital employed, whether realized or unrealized, flowing through the profit and loss account, is similar, although not identical, to the proposals of Baxter (1975) and Edwards, Bell and Johnson (1979). Our claim, however, is not that we have discovered a new system of inflation accounting—clearly we have not—but rather that our theoretical analysis of the conditions under which accounting profitability data would provide relevant information to investors, regulators, and economists about the performance of activities establishes a set of criteria by which the merits of alternative proposals can be assessed.

The intense debate on inflation accounting which took place in the 1970s and early 1980s did not result in RT accounting being adopted in practice, although some more recent signs of a move towards RT accounting can be discerned (see Tweedie and Whittington (1984) for a comprehensive review of developments in inflation accounting). Tweedie and Whittington characterize the course of the inflation accounting debate at the professional level in the English-speaking world as follows. Initially there was widespread support for conventional Constant Purchasing Power (CPP) accounting, in which the historical cost valuation base is adjusted by a general price index.[2] Between 1973 and 1975, CPP proposals appeared in the USA, the UK, Australia, Canada, and New Zealand. But CPP became standard practice in none of these countries—the closest being a Provisional Standard (PSSAP7) in the UK in 1974. The initial support for CPP was followed, in 1975 and 1976, by a 'Current Cost Revolution' in which official bodies in several English-speaking countries moved towards Current Cost accounting (CCA), partly as a result of government influence.[3] Tweedie and Whittington (1984) distinguish two major reasons for this sudden change. One was anxiety by governments concerning the possible destabilising effects of any form of general indexation such as that involved in CPP. The other was anxiety on the part of firms that CPP did not show the true state of affairs as reflected by the specific prices which they faced. The period was one of important relative price changes which CPP, by valuing assets at historic cost adjusted by a general price index, failed to capture.

CCA uses current values for asset valuation and, in its pure form, involves an entity capital maintenance concept which means that capital is adjusted by the specific prices of the assets held by the firm. However, there was considerable controversy over CCA in its pure form, and the professional bodies which were asked to implement it were reluctant to do so. The resulting discussion led to some variant of value to the owner being widely adopted as the current valuation base, and in an attempt to fill the gap left by pure CCA, which takes no account of the losses on holding assets fixed in money value and gains on liabilities fixed in money terms, there were experiments in the UK, New Zealand, and Canada with monetary working capital adjustments (to deal with the former) and gearing adjustments (to deal with the latter) based on changes in the prices of the specific assets held by the firm. The monetary working capital adjustment attempts to extend the concept of the entity beyond its physical assets to its monetary working capital, and applies to initial monetary working capital a specific index which is intended to reflect the change in the firm's need for monetary working capital (in order to maintain its operating capacity) arising from price changes during the period. The gearing adjustment involves the entity approach to maintaining equity capital but a proprietary approach (using money rather than general purchasing power) to long-term borrowing, crediting equity shareholders with an additional profit during a period of inflation as a result of the ownership of the firm shifting from providers of long-term fixed money capital (gearing) to the shareholders. In the form advocated by Godley and Cripps (1975) and Gibbs (1976) the gearing adjustment credits a proportion, equal to the firm's gearing ratio, of all real holding gains to profits. Holding gains on equity-financed assets are not included because the equity capital to be maintained is updated by an index appropriate to the specific assets of the firm. These experiments by no means resolved the controversy, and as a result only the UK has issued a CCA standard (incorporating the two adjustments discussed above)—SSAP16 in 1980. The version of the gearing adjustment adopted in SSAP16 is restricted to apply only to realized holding gains, a development which has been condemned by proponents of the gearing adjustment such as Kennedy (1978) and Gibbs and Seward (1979).

A natural way to reconcile the differences between conventional CPP and pure CCA is to adopt RT accounting, and this was proposed in the UK by the Consultative Committee of Accountancy Bodies (CCAB) in its *Initial Reactions* to the Sandilands Report (1975). But most of the English-speaking world, including the UK, attempted to resolve these differences along the lines of the monetary working capital adjustment and the gearing adjustment. Only in the USA has there been some move towards RT in practice: in 1979 FAS33, issued by the Financial Accounting Standards Board, required companies to report both CCA and CPP profit data, with an element of RT in the reporting of real holding gains and losses. There have also been some limited steps towards RT in more recent proposals for Australia, New Zealand, and Canada, and RT systems were also proposed in the Netherlands in 1976 and Sweden in 1980. But despite these signs of moves towards RT in practice it is clear that this system of accounting has not yet had a significant impact on inflation accounting at the professional level. The most recent official pronouncement on inflation accounting in the UK, the 1984 ED35 'Accounting for Effects of Changing Prices', retains the basic concepts of SSAP16: the changes proposed relate principally to the disclosure requirements of the standard and the companies to which they apply. The only significant change at the level of basic concepts is that a choice of three methods for calculating the gearing adjustment is proposed in ED35: these are the SSAP16 gearing adjustment, which is restricted to realized holding gains only; the Godley–Cripps–Gibbs one, which applies to all holding gains; and a restricted version of what we would regard as the proper gain on borrowing measure, in which a general price index is applied to monetary items not included in monetary working capital.

The superiority of RT over CPP or CCA seems to us to be clear-cut. CPP as conventionally interpreted applies general index adjustment to a historic cost base, and we have argued in detail in the previous chapter that current values, of the value-to-the-owner type, rather than historic costs must be used for assets if information on accounting profitability is to be relevant for economic analysis. Consequently CPP is not a satisfactory system of inflation accounting because of its inappropriate balance sheet conventions. In contrast, CCA, to the extent that it uses value-to-the-owner rules for asset valuation, has precisely those balance sheet conventions which are appropriate for economic interpretations of the accounting rate of return on capital. But the rules applied to the profit and loss account by CCA are inappropriate for such interpretations, because they do not satisfy the basic principle that the whole of any change in the book value of capital should flow through the profit and loss account. CCA in its pure form excludes the holding gain on liabilities and the holding loss on assets fixed in money terms: in the version of CCA that developed subsequently the holding loss on monetary working capital was recognized (albeit via a specific index, reflecting the entity capital maintenance concept of CCA), and some part of the gain on borrowing was incorporated into profit via the gearing adjustment. But the gearing adjustment only recognizes real holding gains as profit to the extent that they are debt-financed (and indeed the UK version in SSAP16 applied the gearing adjustment only to realized holding gains), and it fails to separate the gain on borrowing from holding gains on assets, involving a serious loss of information. The gearing adjustment seems to us to be a confused mixture of entity and proprietary concepts of capital maintenance. We have argued above that the appropriate concept of capital maintenance is a proprietary one, and for this reason, together with its failure to include all changes in the book value of capital in profit, we regard CCA too as an unsatisfactory system of inflation accounting. Both CPP and CCA have certain appealing features, however, and it is quite straightforward to combine them in a CPP adjustment of the CCA value-to-the-owner asset valuation base, with all changes in the book value of capital employed, realized and unrealized, flowing through the profit and loss account. This is the version of RT accounting that we regard as the appropriate system of inflation accounting.

It is useful to spell out the form that this version of inflation accounting would take. Our objective is to use accounting profitability data to derive a real accounting rate of return which can be meaningfully compared with a real cost of capital to give signals to investors and regulators. To show the adjustments to nominal accounting data that are required to allow for inflation we use a simple algebraic example. As the issues involved here do not depend on uncertainty we assume that there is perfect certainty so that no distinction need be made between the *ex ante* and *ex post* accounting rate of return. The nominal accounting rate of return (ARR) on value-to-the-owner conventions over period 1 is given by α where

$$V_0 = \frac{F_1 - K_1 + V_1}{1 + \alpha}. \tag{5.4}$$

Here V_0 is the book value of capital employed at the end of period 0 and V_1 is the book value of capital employed at the end of period 1, both being determined on the basis of the value-to-the-owner rules. F_1 denotes revenue generated during period 1 and K_1 new capital required in period 1. For simplicity all cash flows are assumed to occur at the end of the period. All variables are in nominal terms, i.e. in the current prices of the period by which they are dated. The definition of the ARR in equation 5.4 is directly in terms of net cash flows and initial and final book values of capital: in practice, however, the ARR will probably have to be deduced from accounting profitability data in the manner described in Chapter 3, and we know that this requires accounting profit in period 1 (Y_1) to be defined as

$$Y_1 = F_1 - K_1 + V_1 - V_0 \tag{5.5}$$

while accounting depreciation (D_1) has to satisfy

$$D_1 = K_1 - (V_1 - V_0) \tag{5.6}$$

so that accounting profit can also be written as

$$Y_1 = F_1 - D_1. \tag{5.7}$$

From equation 5.4 the nominal ARR is given as

$$\alpha = \frac{F_1 - K_1 + V_1 - V_0}{V_0} \tag{5.8}$$

which can, using equations 5.5 and 5.7, also be expressed as

$$\alpha = \frac{Y_1}{V_0} \tag{5.9}$$

or

$$\alpha = \frac{F_1 - D_1}{V_0}. \tag{5.10}$$

We know from the analysis of Chapter 4 that a comparison of the nominal ARR obtained in this way with the nominal cost of capital, ρ, is a valid way of assessing the performance of the activity in question.

How can a real ARR be measured in order for comparisons with the real cost of capital, r, to be made? The relationship between the nominal and real costs of capital is given by

$$(1 + \rho) = (1 + r)(1 + \pi)$$

where π is the rate of inflation over a period, measured by the increase in some general price index over the period, so that

$$\rho = r(1 + \pi) + \pi. \tag{5.11}$$

It follows that the nominal ARR is related to the real ARR, a, as follows

$$\alpha = a(1 + \pi) + \pi. \tag{5.12}$$

Substituting for α in equation 5.8 from 5.12 and rearranging, we find that

$$a = \frac{F_1 - K_1 + V_1 - (1 + \pi)V_0}{(1 + \pi)V_0}. \tag{5.13}$$

Alternatively, substituting in equation 5.10 from 5.12,

$$a = \frac{F_1 - D_1 - \pi V_0}{(1 + \pi)V_0}. \tag{5.14}$$

The numerators of the right-hand side of equations 5.13 and 5.14 are two alternative ways of writing the same inflation-adjusted profit figure. The required adjustment to nominal accounting profits is simply the subtraction of πV_0, the inflation rate times the initial book value of capital employed, from nominal accounting profit. Equations 5.13 and 5.14 show that in order to derive the real ARR, real (inflation-adjusted) accounting profits must be divided by the initial book value of capital employed expressed in constant (end-period) prices, $(1 + \pi)V_0$.

The various inflation adjustments which are required to be made to nominal accounting profits can be seen more easily if we write the book value of capital employed in terms of its constituent parts: at any date t

$$V_t = G_t + S_t + M_t - L_t \qquad (5.15)$$

where G_t is the value of fixed assets at t, S_t the value of stocks, M_t the value of net monetary assets held, and L_t the value of outstanding liabilities at t. In each case the value of these items in the balance sheet is established using the value-to-the-owner base. This raises the question of how the value-to-the-owner rules apply to these different assets and liabilities. Clearly there is no distinction to be made between present value (PV), replacement cost (RC), and net realizable value (NRV) for net monetary assets which have a clearly defined money value. It is also probable that for many types of stocks, buying and selling prices will not differ and hence the current market price of stocks can be used to obtain the value to the owner, although this is unlikely to be the case for work in progress, in which market dealings are rare so that neither a buying nor a selling price exists and hence a choice between PV, RC, and NRV has to be made in the same way as for fixed assets. As far as liabilities are concerned, these can be valued by a straightforward adaptation of the rules used to value assets, as suggested by Baxter (1975).[4] The value of a liability under value-to-the-owner rules is given by

Value of the liability = max {Replacement loan, Net payments to meet the liability}

where

Net payments to meet the liability = min {PV of future payments, Current repurchase price}

For long-term fixed interest loans, for example, the current repurchase price is the call price, and the replacement cost is the amount borrowed inclusive of transactions costs. The PV of future payments is then computed at the cost of capital associated with the replacement loan.

We can now give a simple analysis of the inflation adjustments that must be made to nominal accounting profits in order to arrive at real accounting profits. Suppose that at time t, a firm's assets and liabilities comprise:

(a) g_t units of a single fixed asset which decays at the rate δ per period, so that if the firm does not purchase any new units of this asset in the subsequent period it will hold only $(1 - \delta)g_t$ units at time $t + 1$. We assume that the market price at which units of the asset can be bought at t is p_t, and that the value-to-the-owner rules lead to replacement cost valuation of the fixed asset so that p_t is the price used to value the firm's holding of this asset.

(b) s_t units of a single type of stock which can be bought or sold at a market price q_t, and hence are valued at this price. The entire stock held at time t is assumed to be used up during the subsequent period.

(c) net monetary assets with a money value m_t.

(d) l_t outstanding bonds each with a current market price b_t which is therefore used to value this liability.

The book value of capital at the end of period t (equivalent to the beginning of period $t+1$) is therefore

$$V_t = p_t g_t + q_t s_t + m_t - b_t l_t. \tag{5.16}$$

Inflation-adjusted profit $\bar{Y}_t$ is

$$\bar{Y}_t = F_t - K_t + V_t - (1+\pi)V_{t-1}. \tag{5.17}$$

Consider period 1 (which lasts from $t=0$ to $t=1$), and assume that all transactions and cash flows occur at the end of the period. In terms of the assets and liabilities held by the firm, K_1 can be written as

$$K_1 = p_1(g_1 - (1-\delta)g_0) + q_1 s_1 + (m_1 - m_0) - b_1(l_1 - l_0). \tag{5.18}$$

Substituting equations 5.16 and 5.18 into 5.17 and rearranging yields the following expression for inflation-adjusted profit:

$$\begin{aligned} \bar{Y}_1 = {} & F_1 - p_1 \delta g_0 + (p_1 - (1+\pi)p_0)g_0 - (1+\pi)q_0 s_0 - \pi m_0 \\ & - (b_1 - (1+\pi)b_0)l_0. \end{aligned} \tag{5.19}$$

Equation 5.19 shows clearly the various steps that are involved in obtaining the real terms accounting profit figure which we regard as the appropriate one if inflation-adjusted accounting profitability data is to be useful for economic analysis. Revenues received, F_1, are adjusted as follows:

(i) a term $p_1 \delta g_0$ is subtracted, reflecting the current (replacement cost) value of the decay of the stock of the fixed asset over the period.

(ii) a term $(p_1 - (1+\pi)p_0)g_0$ is added, reflecting real holding gains or losses on the stock of fixed asset held at the start of the period. There is a real holding gain if $p_1 > (1+\pi)p_0$, so that the buying price of the fixed asset has risen by more than the rate of inflation over the period, and a real holding loss if $p_1 < (1+\pi)p_0$, so that the buying price of the fixed asset has increased by less than the inflation rate. If $p_1 = (1+\pi)p_0$ there is no adjustment as there is neither a real holding gain nor a loss. It should be emphasized that the particular forms taken by both the adjustment for the decay in the stock of the fixed asset and the adjustment for real holding gains or losses on fixed assets in equation 5.19 are a result of the assumption made for this illustration that the value-to-the-owner rules lead to replacement cost valuation at time 0 and time 1. Although it has been argued that the value-to-the-owner base is likely to be replacement cost in most circumstances (Gee and Peasnell (1976)), it cannot be assumed that the value-to-the-owner rules will always result in RC valuations. If the stock of the fixed asset were to be valued at replacement cost at time 0 and at net realizable value at time 1, and the selling price of the fixed asset at time 1 were to be d_1, the adjustment for decay would become

$d_1 \delta g_0$—the value of the decay would be given by current sale (NRV) prices—and the real holding gain or loss adjustment would be $(d_1 - (1 + \pi)p_0)g_0$—there would be a real holding loss if $d_1 < (1 + \pi)p_0$, and conversely a gain if $d_1 > (1 + \pi)p_0$.

(iii) a term $(1 + \pi)q_0 s_0$ is subtracted, reflecting stock appreciation over the period. The caveats mentioned above with respect to the precise form of the adjustment shown in equation 5.19 also apply to the stock appreciation adjustment, but in general there is less scope for PV, RC, and NRV valuations of stocks to differ than is the case with fixed assets.

(iv) a term πm_0 is subtracted, reflecting the real holding loss on net monetary assets held at the start of the period.

(v) a term $(b_1 - (1 + \pi)b_0)l_0$ is subtracted, reflecting the change over the period in the real value of the firm's liabilities. If $b_1 = b_0$, so that the current market price of the firm's bonds is unchanged over the period, this adjustment reduces to the addition of $\pi b_0 l_0$, the gain on borrowing as it is conventionally called. Note that this case of constancy in the market price includes the one where the firm's liabilities are fixed in money terms. But in general this adjustment will take a more complex form because there will be gains or losses due to changes in the market price of bonds as well as the gain resulting from inflationary erosion of the real value of outstanding debt.

The above analysis has shown, by means of a simple algebraic example, how a real accounting rate of return is measured and the adjustments which have to be made in order to arrive at a real terms profit figure using value to the owner as the current valuation base. We must emphasize that the particular valuations used in the example are not to be interpreted as the universally appropriate ones. The purpose of the example was to illustrate the inflation adjustments implied by our version of Real Terms accounting, and to that end it was based on the specific assumption that the value-to-the-owner rules resulted in RC values for the fixed asset and market price valuation for stocks and liabilities.

5.4 Conclusion

In this chapter we have argued in favour of a particular version of a form of inflation accounting which has a distinguished intellectual history—Real Terms accounting. This form of inflation accounting combines a current valuation basis for capital employed with general index adjustment of capital for the effects of inflation. The specific version of RT accounting that we advocate uses value to the owner as the current valuation basis, and also requires all changes in the book value of capital employed between any two dates, reflecting both relative price changes and general inflation, to flow through the profit and loss account for the intervening period. Our reason for advocating this particular version of RT accounting is that it emerges naturally from our discussion in the previous chapter as the appropriate way in which to measure real accounting profitability if the resulting information is to provide economists, investors, regulators, and others with appropriate signals about the performance of activities.

The discussion in this chapter has, together with much of the whole debate on inflation accounting, been conducted at a theoretical level, and it is natural to ask whether the different methods of inflation accounting lead to significant differences in accounting profitability in practice. In the next chapter we turn to an investigation of the quantitative significance of the differences between accounting profitability measures based on CPP, CCA, and RT approaches, which will help to bring out the importance of some of the theoretical points discussed in this chapter.

Notes

1. See Whittington (1983) ch. 6 for a full discussion of these capital maintenance concepts.
2. The conventional interpretation of CPP as applying a general index adjustment to the historical cost base is a rather narrow interpretation of CPP, which can be applied to current value bases, and this is, of course, what RT accounting does. CPP is, however, generally interpreted in this narrow sense.
3. These were the Securities and Exchange Commission in the USA with its ASR190 replacement cost disclosures (announced in 1975); the Mathews Report in the Committee of Inquiry into Inflation and Taxation (1975) in Australia; the Sandilands Report (1975) in the UK; and the Richardson Report (1976) in New Zealand.
4. Baxter suggests that, symmetrically with the idea that the value-to-the-owner rules give the minimum loss that a firm would suffer if deprived of an asset, the value-to-the-owner rules should, when applied to liabilities, give the maximum gain that a firm would receive if it were relieved of the liability.

6

Inflation Accounting II
Alternative Profitability Measures

6.1 Introduction

IN this chapter we illustrate the quantitative significance of the differences between CPP, CCA, and RT measures of accounting profitability, firstly by examining the profitability figures that the three approaches produce under various hypothetical situations, and secondly by estimating CPP, CCA, and RT profitability figures for a sample of British companies over the period 1966–81. We also include historic cost (HC) profitability figures in these illustrations in order to compare the various inflation-adjusted measures with what remains the most widely used accounting profit measure. In these illustrations the version of CCA that we use is that introduced in the UK as a statement of standard accounting practice in 1980—SSAP16, Current Cost Accounting—modified by the use of replacement cost as the asset valuation method instead of value to the owner as prescribed in SSAP16. Similarly the version of RT accounting used in the following illustrations is not exactly the one we recommend as it too uses replacement cost rather than value to the owner as the asset valuation base. This substitution of replacement cost for value to the owner as the current valuation basis is made necessary by the fact that we simply do not possess the information to establish asset values on the value-to-the-owner rules. It can be argued that the value-to-the-owner rules will result in the use of replacement cost in many circumstances, so that the RT profitability figures reported below might be justified as a good approximation to the inflation-adjusted accounting profitability measure which we regard as being relevant for economic analysis, but the purpose of the exercise in this chapter is not to produce 'correct' accounting profitability figures—indeed we wish to make clear that the following measures are not to be interpreted in this way—rather it is to *illustrate* the differences between various approaches, and for this purpose it does not matter that replacement cost is used instead of value to the owner as the asset valuation base.

A crucial part in the following illustrations is played by the Institute for Fiscal Studies inflation accounting model, which uses a company's published historic cost accounting data to estimate its inflation-adjusted accounts. This model is described in detail by Mayer (1982) and Meadowcroft (1983). The major practical difficulty in using historic cost information to produce inflation-adjusted accounts arises from the need to estimate the length of life of a firm's capital stock and to have a historical record of past investments over this lifetime in order to revalue depreciation and capital employed from historic cost to current prices. Indeed if, as is highly probable, firms have heterogeneous capital stocks then different life-times and depreciation rates have to be established and appropriate price indices have to be applied to the various components of past investments: the paucity of information on the composition of company investments, however, means that this complication has not been considered, and is another reason why the figures to be reported should only be regarded as illustrative. The average length of life of fixed assets (buildings, plant and machinery, and vehicles) obtained from company accounts and used by the model in its computation of inflation adjustments is seventeen years: this is substantially less than the service times employed by the Central Statistical Office in the determination of National Accounts valuations of capital consumption and replacement cost capital stocks (the average CSO length of life of fixed assets for the entire corporate sector is just under forty years). The reasons for preferring the shorter estimate, and possible explanations for the difference between the two, are discussed in Mayer and Meadowcroft (1984). A number of other technical issues are raised in inflation-adjusting historic cost accounts: takeovers, for example, seriously distort the time profile of a company's gross investment, while revaluations of past investments already included in reported statements threaten to introduce an element of double counting. The way in which the model corrects for these complications is discussed in Meadowcroft (1983); inevitably a number of heroic assumptions have to be made, but the model attempts to incorporate available information in as systematic a fashion as possible.

The inflation accounting model produces estimates of CPP profit and loss statements and balance sheets by applying movements in the Retail Price Index (RPI) to the average of opening and closing stocks and net monetary assets (defined as cash, marketable securities, and net trade debtors less bank overdrafts and loans, long-term liabilities, and dividend, interest and tax liabilities) and revaluing historic cost investments by the RPI to give CPP depreciation and capital employed. Estimates of accounts on a CCA basis are given by revaluing historic cost investments by the plant and machinery and building price deflators implicit in the National Accounts 'Blue Book' capital expenditure figures, weighted together by the investment proportions of the main industry in which the firm in question is operating. This enables current depreciation and capital employed to be stated on a replacement cost basis. The adjustments for stock appreciation (called the 'cost of sales adjustment' in CCA terminology) and monetary working capital are made by applying the Wholesale Price Index (WPI) of materials and fuel and output of manufactured products weighted together by aggregate stock proportions to the average of opening and closing stocks and monetary working capital (defined as cash plus net trade debtors) respectively. The gearing adjustment then abates the other corrections (for depreciation, stock appreciation, and monetary working capital) by the proportion of capital employed which takes the form of debt (essentially all net monetary liabilities that have not been included in monetary working capital). Finally, estimates of RT accounts are produced by making a monetary adjustment which is identical to the CPP correction, a depreciation adjustment which is identical to the CCA correction, revaluing depreciation to current replacement cost, and recording fixed assets on the balance sheet at replacement cost. But the real value of capital which has to be maintained before a profit is recognized is given by applying the increase in the RPI to initial capital at replacement cost, so that RT profit includes real holding gains and losses on fixed assets to the extent that the change in the weighted implicit deflators for plant and machinery and buildings differs from that in the RPI. Similarly stocks are revalued to current replacement cost on the balance sheet, as in CCA, but the stock appreciation adjustment is given by applying the change in the RPI over the accounting year to the average of opening and closing replacement cost stocks.[1] Assets are thus shown at replacement cost but the inflationary erosion of their value is related to the RPI rather than to a specific price index. A feature of these RT accounts that should be noted is that long-term liabilities are treated as having a fixed monetary value: as was made clear in Section 5.3 of the previous chapter, however, we regard the appropriate valuation of such liabilities as being in terms of market prices. Data limitations prevent us adopting this valuation method in the RT estimates presented.

6.2 Simple examples of the differences between various approaches to inflation accounting

In this section we consider the differences between the various methods of accounting in a number of highly simplified examples. We begin with that shown in Table 6.1, the first column of which gives the historic cost accounts of an 'average' quoted firm operating in the first half of the 1970s. It has been derived from the aggregate profit and loss statements and balance sheets shown in *Business Monitor* for the years 1970–4, but has been altered in one fundamental respect for reasons which will become self-evident—dividends have been increased to the full level of profits so that retentions are assumed to be equal to zero. These accounts will be associated with 1972, and it is assumed that there has been no inflation before 1972 and that this company has been in a stationary state, with constant real gross profit, real depreciation, real assets and liabilities, etc., for a long time. In these circumstances the HC accounts correctly measure capital employed, capital expenditure required to maintain the constancy of the physical assets employed, etc.; measured on end-year shareholders' capital and reserves the company earned an impressive real rate of return in 1972 of $4162/19500 = 21.3$ per cent.

Now suppose that in 1973 the activities of the firm remain unchanged, but all prices are 10 per cent higher as is the return on all monetary assets and

Table 6.1. Inflation adjustments for a set of accounts for a firm with unchanged real behaviour and a 10 per cent rise in prices between 1972 and 1973

	Accounts (£000)			
	1972	1973 HC	1973 CPP/RT	1973 CCA
Gross income (net of interest and taxes)	5 631	6 403	6 403	6 403
Current depreciation	1 469	1 469	1 469	1 469
Dividends	4 162	4 578	4 578	4 578
Inflation corrections	—	—	− 356	− 938
Retained profit	0	356	0	− 582
Assets				
Trade debtors and cash	13 001	14 301	14 301	14 301
Marketable securities	2 348	2 583	2 583	2 583
Stocks	11 341	12 475	12 475	12 475
Net fixed assets	17 411	17 558†	19 152	19 152
TOTAL ASSETS	44 101	46 917	48 511	48 511
Liabilities				
Trade creditors	11 043	12 147	12 147	12 147
Other liabilities	13 558	14 914	14 914	14 914
Shareholder capital and reserves	19 500	19 856	21 450	21 450††
TOTAL LIABILITIES	44 101	46 917	48 511	48 511
Adjustments to HC profits required by different inflation accounting methods				
Stock appreciation	—	—	1 134	1 134
Depreciation adjustment	—	—	147	147
Monetary loss	—	—	− 925	—
Monetary working capital adjustment	—	—	—	196
Gearing adjustment	—	—	—	539
TOTAL INFLATION ADJUSTMENT	—	—	356	938

† This increase of 147 over the 1972 figure reflects the HC provision of 1469 against investment of 1616 which is made to maintain the physical assets employed constant.
†† Including CCA reserves.

liabilities. For simplicity it is assumed that the HC values of all monetary assets and liabilities correspond to the current ones: this can be rationalized by thinking of the firm acquiring a completely new set of such assets and liabilities in 1973. Column 2 of Table 6.1 shows that HC earnings rise in consequence by 18.5 per cent (as the HC depreciation provision is unchanged), so that if real dividends are maintained, the firm reports HC retained profits of £356 000 and

HC shareholders' capital and reserves of £19 856 000—a rise in nominal terms but a fall in real terms. The HC rate of return is 24.8 per cent.

In this example, with just a general rise in prices, there is no difference between CPP and RT accounts, which are shown in column 3 of Table 6.1. The adjustments which have to be made to the HC accounts are as follows: first, fixed assets are revalued to 1973 prices in the balance sheet; second, the HC depreciation provision has to be augmented by £147 000 to reflect the investment of £1 616 000 (= £1 469 000 × 1.1) which is required to maintain the physical assets employed constant; third, a provision of £1 134 000 (= £11 341 000 × 0.1) for stock appreciation has to be subtracted; and fourthly an overall gain on monetary assets (shown as a negative loss in the table) of £925 000 (= £(11 043 000 + 13 558 000 − 13 001 000 − 2 348 000) × 0.1) has to be added. The overall correction reduces CPP/RT profits to £4 578 000 and the rate of return is correctly measured as 21.3 per cent on an unchanged real shareholders' capital of £21 450 000.

Column 4 of Table 6.1 shows the CCA accounts for 1973. The revaluation of fixed assets, stock appreciation adjustment, and depreciation adjustment are the same as for CPP and RT. The differences lie in the monetary working capital adjustment (MWCA) of £196 000 (= £(13 001 000 − 11 043 000) × 0.1) and the gearing adjustment of £539 000 (= £(1 134 000 + 147 000 + 196 000) × ([14 914 − 2 583]/[14 914 − 2 583 + 21 450])) which produce a total CCA monetary adjustment of −£343 000. As a result CCA profits are some 13 per cent lower than CPP/RT ones, at £3 996 000, so that if an unchanged real dividend is paid retentions are −£582 000 thus reducing shareholders' capital (excluding CCA reserves) to £20 868 000 and the CCA rate of return is 3 996/20 868 = 19.1 per cent. CCA profits and profitability differ from the correct CPP/RT figures even in this simple case where there is no history of inflation, merely a step change in prices.

The reason for this discrepancy is simply that the gearing adjustment and the MWCA do not incorporate all monetary adjustments in a systematic fashion. Those items not covered by the MWCA are included in the gearing adjustment but only with reference to the inflation adjustments made elsewhere. In particular, the gearing adjustment is related to the depreciation adjustment which is in turn dependent on a long past history of inflation rates. If inflation has historically been low in relation to its current level then the gearing adjustment will be small on account of the relatively low depreciation correction, and inflation adjusted profits will be understated. This is precisely the situation that is being described in Table 6.1 where inflation was historically zero and suddenly rose to 10 per cent. Similarly if inflation is currently lower than it has been in the recent past then the gearing adjustment will be large due to the relatively large depreciation correction and inflation adjusted profits will be overstated.

We provide a further illustration of this point by assuming that our hypothetical 'average' company's accounts had remained constant in nominal terms at their 1972 level from 1948 onwards and will continue to do so indefinitely subsequent to 1972, while all prices rose at a constant rate of 5 per cent per annum until 1972 and 20 per cent thereafter. The resulting rates of return under HC, CPP/RT (as in the previous example these two methods give the same answer) and CCA are shown in Table 6.2. The HC rate of return is constant at 21.3 per cent throughout, but this is now a nominal return on an undervalued shareholders' equity capital. Following the rise in the inflation rate in 1972 the CPP/RT rate of return falls smoothly to its new steady-state value of −8.5 per cent (column 2 in Table 6.2). But, since the gearing adjustment in CCA is based on depreciation adjustments which depend on inflation over the previous seventeen years (the assumed average length of life of the capital stock), when the increase in inflation occurs the gearing adjustment is in large part determined by the previous 5 per cent inflation rate. Hence the gearing adjustment is understated and CCA profitability lies substantially below CPP/RT profitability immediately after the increase. But as the influence of the 5 per cent inflation rate on the depreciation adjustment fades so too does the discrepancy between CCA and CPP/RT profitability, and the CCA rate of return eventually tends to a steady-state value of −9.1 per cent. The short-run transition of CCA profitability is thus seriously distorted by the gearing adjustment's dependence on past inflation rates, and even in the long-run there remains a small discrepancy which depends on the relationship between the depreciation adjustment and the decline in the real value of physical assets as a consequence of inflation.[2]

Table 6.2. Constant nominal accounts, 5 per cent inflation to 1972, 20 per cent inflation thereafter

	HC (%)	CPP/RT (%)	CCA (%)
1970	21.3	12.9	12.6
1971	21.3	12.9	12.6
1972	21.3	13.0	12.7
1973	21.3	9.3	5.9
1974	21.3	6.8	3.9
1975	21.3	5.0	2.4
1976	21.3	3.4	1.1
1977	21.3	2.0	−0.1
1978	21.3	0.7	−1.1
1979	21.3	−0.5	−2.1
1980	21.3	−1.6	−3.1
1981	21.3	−2.6	−4.0

Note: The slight rise in 1972 for CPP/RT and CCA profitability figures is due to a timing difference between the revaluations of end of year balance sheet entries and mid-year profit and loss items.

While the gearing adjustment is an important reason for the differences between CCA, CPP, and RT profit measures it is not the only one. CCA employs a specific price index in the determination of monetary adjustments while CPP and RT use a general consumer price index. To illustrate the significance of this we return to our original example of constant real accounts and suppose that between 1972 and 1973 there had been a 10 per cent rise in the price of stocks and fixed assets (and the costs of producing them) but that other prices remained unchanged so that these increases were real ones relative to consumer prices. Table 6.3 shows the accounts for this situation under the various approaches. Column 1 gives HC accounts for 1973: there is no change in HC profit but in the balance sheet end-year stocks are valued at £12 475 000 reflecting their higher cost of purchase, while there is also a small increase in the HC value of fixed assets reflecting the difference between the depreciation provision and the cost of maintaining fixed assets employed constant. The HC value of shareholders' capital therefore rises and HC profitability falls to $4\,162/20\,781 = 20.0$ per cent. The expenditure on new capital goods which is needed to maintain fixed assets constant exceeds the HC depreciation provision by £147 000: a correct depreciation charge requires the restatement of the accounts on a RT basis (column 2) with depreciation raised by £147 000 to reflect the 10 per cent increase in the price of capital goods. It is also necessary to allow for the higher cost of replacing stocks with a stock appreciation provision of £1 134 000. But set against these are the real holding gains on the fixed assets and stocks already in the possession of the firm, so that RT profit is £5 756 000. In the balance sheet both stocks and fixed assets are valued at current (1973) prices, so shareholders' capital is £22 375 000 and RT profitability is $5\,756/22\,375 = 25.7$ per cent. It should be noted that the adjustments made to HC accounts to reach RT ones have nothing to do with inflation—they are merely the appropriate responses to the relative price changes. There is no general inflation in this example. As a result the accounts in this example given by CPP, which simply adjusts HC accounts by the movements in a general price index, are identical to the HC ones: CPP fails to take account of the rise in the price of stocks and fixed assets in either the profit and loss account or the balance sheet.

The CCA accounts for this example (column 4 of Table 6.3) are, however, radically different not only from the HC ones but also from the RT accounts. CCA makes the same balance sheet, stock appreciation and depreciation adjustments as RT, but it also makes a MWCA of £196 000 by applying the 10 per cent rise in stock prices to net trade debtors and cash, and it then abates the stock appreciation, depreciation and MWCA corrections by a gearing adjustment of £493 000. The result is that CCA profits are £3 178 000 and CCA profitability is $3\,178/22\,375 = 14.2$ per cent, both substantially below the RT figures.

The reasons for this understatement of profitability by CCA are clear. While it is correctly revaluing fixed assets and the depreciation adjustment to current

Table 6.3. Adjustments for a set of accounts reflecting constant real activities and a 10 per cent rise in the price of stocks and fixed assets between 1972 and 1973

	Accounts (£000)			
	1973 HC	1973 RT	1973 CPP	1973 CCA
Gross income (net of interest and taxes)	5 631	5 631	5 631	5 631
Current depreciation	1 469	1 469	1 469	1 469
Dividends	4 162	4 162	4 162	4 162
Price-change corrections	—	1 594	—	−984
Retained profit	0	1 594	0	−984
Assets				
Trade debtors and cash	13 001	13 001	13 001	13 001
Marketable securities	2 348	2 348	2 348	2 348
Stocks	12 475	12 475	12 475	12 475
Net fixed assets	17 558	19 152	17 558	19 152
TOTAL ASSETS	45 382	46 976	45 382	46 976
Liabilities				
Trade creditors	11 043	11 043	11 043	11 043
Other liabilities	13 558	13 558	13 558	13 558
Shareholder capital and reserves	20 781	22 375	20 781	22 375
TOTAL LIABILITIES	45 382	46 976	45 382	46 976
Price-change adjustments				
Stock appreciation	—	1 134	—	1 134
Depreciation adjustments	—	147	—	147
Monetary working capital adjustment	—	—	—	196
Gearing adjustment	—	—	—	−493
Holding gain on stocks	—	−1 134	—	—
Holding gain on fixed assets	—	−1 741	—	—
TOTAL PRICE-CHANGE ADJUSTMENT	—	−1 594	—	984

cost and adjusting for stock appreciation, CCA is failing to recognize the holding gain on fixed assets and stocks. It is therefore suggesting that a rise in the price of assets under the possession of investors in the firm does not make them better off. This is both counterintuitive and wrong. Capital gains are earnings analogous to the trading profits that the firm is generating, and whilst the gains might be more volatile than normal trading returns this in no way undermines their inclusion in the profit and loss account. It may be appropriate to draw investors' attention to the volatility of earnings in the form of capital gains (or losses) on assets owned by the firm, but it is not appropriate to exclude them.

This confusion, which results from the entity concept of capital maintenance on which CCA is based, also pervades the monetary adjustments. It is quite inappropriate for the MWCA to be based on specific stock prices. Why should £100 cash in the possession of the firm in 1972 be worth £90 in 1973 prices when all that has changed is the price of stocks and fixed assets? Since not many shareholders regularly purchase such goods their prices would appear to be of little relevance in computing the value of cash retained in the firm. Exactly the same objections apply to the gearing adjustment, which attempts to reflect shareholders' gain on borrowing but does so by abating the adjustments for stock appreciation, depreciation, and monetary working capital and hence relates the gain to movements in specific prices. The gain on borrowing in money terms to shareholders as a result of a rise in the price of bulldozers is not easy to discern. In the example of Table 6.3 the error resulting from the gearing adjustment attributing borrowing gains as a result of the rise in the relative price of stocks and fixed assets partially offsets the errors from excluding holding gains and including a loss on monetary working capital due to the relative price increase, but the overall conclusion to be drawn from this example is that CCA creates a great deal of confusion even in the absence of general inflation.

The differences between CCA, CPP, and RT can be illustrated in a different way by computing the annual adjustment to accounts that relative price movements would have created in the absence of general inflation had profit and loss and balance sheet statements remained at their 1972 level in nominal terms from 1948 onwards. This time we have taken the actual relative price changes of stocks and capital goods between 1966 and 1981 but have assumed that there was no underlying inflation so that consumer prices remained constant. Thus, as explained above, there is no CPP correction and CPP rates of return in Table 6.4 (column 2) are identical to the HC return of 21.3 per cent (column 1). In contrast CCA profitability displays some dramatic movements. These are primarily a consequence of changes in stock prices: falls in real stock prices in 1968 and 1970 augmented CCA profitability by introducing negative stock and monetary working capital adjustments, while the commodity price booms of 1973 and 1974, 1976 and 1979[3] significantly diminished CCA rates of return. The restatement of depreciation at replacement cost also affected the CCA figures, but not as appreciably as the stock price movements. Falling real plant and machinery prices over much of the period raised the CCA rate of return but the annual fluctuations are largely a consequence of volatile stock prices. The magnitude of these stock appreciation adjustments alerts us to the importance of including holding gains on stocks and choosing an appropriate price basis for monetary corrections. The RT figures, shown in column 4 of Table 6.4, do just that, and it can be seen that RT profitability in this example

Table 6.4. Constant nominal accounts, no inflation, actual
movements in relative prices between 1966 and 1981

	HC (%)	CPP (%)	CCA (%)	RT (%)
1966	21.3	21.3	23.0	21.7
1967	21.3	21.3	22.2	21.8
1968	21.3	21.3	23.2	21.9
1969	21.3	21.3	22.8	21.8
1970	21.3	21.3	23.0	21.7
1971	21.3	21.3	23.7	21.7
1972	21.3	21.3	21.4	21.8
1973	21.3	21.3	15.0	21.8
1974	21.3	21.3	18.0	21.9
1975	21.3	21.3	23.7	21.8
1976	21.3	21.3	19.2	21.7
1977	21.3	21.3	24.4	21.7
1978	21.3	21.3	23.5	21.7
1979	21.3	21.3	21.6	22.1
1980	21.3	21.3	26.6	22.5
1981	21.3	21.3	24.2	22.6

is far more stable from year to year than CCA, while being consistently a little
above the HC/CPP figures. The combined effect of revaluing depreciation and
stocks used to current costs, together with inclusion of real holding gains and
losses on assets and the exclusion of spurious monetary gains or losses
resulting from specific price changes, is to produce a profitability figure which
does take account of relative price movements but is not highly sensitive to
them. In contrast CCA, which includes specific price effects in monetary gains
and losses, exaggerates the effects of relative price movements on profitability.
Table 6.4 therefore demonstrates that the choice of an index with which to
deflate book values and cash flows is of much less significance than a
systematic application of inflation corrections.

To summarize, these simple examples have illustrated the ways in which
both CPP and CCA differ from RT, which we regard as the appropriate
method of inflation accounting. CPP fails to revalue capital goods to current
replacement cost and so, in general, produces an inappropriate depreciation
figure and does not include real holding gains and losses. The monetary
correction under CPP is, however, appropriate (although this conclusion
depends on the assumption made in the above examples that liabilities have a
value which is fixed in money terms). The two characteristic features of CCA,
its financial correction and its use of specific prices in defining the capital to be
maintained intact, have been seen to create severe distortions. The

combination of the MWCA and the gearing adjustment produce a financial correction which is sensitive to the allocation of items between the two components and to the history of past inflation. Specific prices are inappropriate for measuring the loss on monetary assets and the gain on borrowing while their use in defining capital to be maintained intact eliminates real holding gains on stocks and capital goods which should be included in profit.

6.3 Illustrative inflation adjustments for a sample of UK firms

In this section we use the IFS Inflation Accounting model to calculate estimates of accounts on CPP, CCA, and RT bases over the period 1966–81 from published (HC) accounts for each of a group of 160 firms registered (and primarily operating) in the UK. The resulting profitability estimates should be regarded as no more than illustrative of the differences between the various systems of inflation accounting, not only for the reasons mentioned in Section 6.1, but for several others as well. In particular we had to link together two different sources of published accounting data. In order to produce inflation-adjusted accounts it is necessary to have a long run of annual accounts, because, as has already been discussed, the depreciation adjustment requires investment information for at least seventeen years prior to the year in question. There is only one database in the UK which provides a sufficiently long run of accounting information—the data bank assembled by the Department of Industry (DI) and standardized by the Department of Applied Economics (DAE) at Cambridge University. Unfortunately this database is currently only available to 1977 so that to produce results for more recent years it had to be linked with information provided by Datastream. There are considerable difficulties involved in linking together accounting series from different sources. Definitions, degrees of disaggregation, and methods of standardization vary, and while considerable efforts have been made to ensure as great a degree of consistency as possible, some series are impossible to match. This should be borne in mind when examining the results, which for 1966–75 are based on DI/DAE data and for 1976–81 on Datastream data. It was only possible to find data on 160 companies which had a complete record from 1948 to 1981 and were included on both the DI/DAE and Datastream original data sources. The resulting group of firms for which inflation-adjusted accounts have been estimated spans the main industrial classifications but cannot be regarded as a representative sample of UK industrial and commercial companies in terms of size or industry. Nevertheless, although the sample concentrates on relatively large firms, there is no reason to suppose that the conclusions about the effects of different inflation adjustments are systematically biased as a consequence.

Table 6.5 shows the average (across the 160 firms, weighted by opening shareholders' capital and reserves) estimate of HC, CPP, CCA, and RT annual

Table 6.5. Accounting rates of return 1966–81

Year	HC (%)	CPP (%)	CCA (%)	RT (%)
1966	7.3	4.1	5.0	4.5
1967	9.4	6.4	6.3	7.0
1968	11.5	7.2	8.0	8.0
1969	12.5	7.7	7.8	8.5
1970	12.5	7.1	7.3	7.7
1971	12.6	6.2	6.6	6.6
1972	15.6	8.4	6.1	8.7
1973	17.4	8.2	−2.9	8.2
1974	15.0	3.9	−2.1	4.0
1975	14.3	−0.3	−3.3	−0.1
1976	22.9	6.1	1.1	6.3
1977	20.6	4.4	6.8	4.7
1978	19.9	5.6	5.9	5.9
1979	18.5	3.3	0.2	3.9
1980	13.6	−1.0	0.3	0.1
1981	13.4	−0.3	−0.5	1.3
AVERAGE	14.8	4.8	3.3	5.3

accounting rates of return for the period 1966–81. The rate of return is defined as earnings (after tax, interest, and depreciation) on shareholders' capital and reserves. Earnings include both trading and investment income, and tax is based on stated amounts in company accounts.[4] Shareholders' reserves exclude goodwill. It is no surprise to observe the great difference between HC profitability in column 1 and the three inflation-adjusted profitability estimates in the other columns. One particularly interesting feature of the inflation-adjusted estimates in relation to their HC counterpart is the magnitude of the corrections in 1977 and 1978 when inflation was relatively low following the very high rates of 1974 and 1975. The reason for this is that the depreciation adjustment and revaluation of capital employed depend on the extent to which past investment expenditures have been revalued since acquisition, and so any change in prices will continue to create an adjustment to depreciation and capital employed as long as capital assets purchased before the price change are still being employed. These adjustments will reflect a weighted average of past rates of inflation and so may go on rising even if inflation is falling. Since fixed assets typically have a long service life (our estimate is that the average life of assets is seventeen years) a period of high inflation will involve significant adjustments to depreciation and capital employed for many years after it has passed. The rapid inflation of the late 1970s and early 1980s will continue to create significant inflation adjustments for several years to come, and the implications for the use of HC profitability figures in the latter half of the 1980s, even if the annual rate of inflation fades, are clear.

The other striking feature of Table 6.5 concerns the relations between the CPP, CCA, and RT profitability estimates. CPP and RT rates of return are very similar, with RT profitability being slightly above CPP in every year except 1973 (when the two are equal): this is what would be expected, given the results of Table 6.4, which show that the effect of excluding relative price changes in CPP profitability and including them in RT is, with the actual relative price movements over 1966–81, consistently to raise RT profitability above CPP. But the CCA rate of return diverges sharply from the other two inflation-adjusted ones in some years, particularly 1973, 1974, and 1979. The analysis in the previous section suggests why this might be so. On average CCA profitability lies below CPP and RT profitability, and this is precisely what we would have predicted on the basis of Tables 6.1 and 6.2 in a period in which inflation had substantially increased—the gearing adjustment includes monetary adjustments not covered by the MWCA only with reference to other inflation adjustments, and the relatively small depreciation correction which results when inflation is currently high relative to its historical level means that the gearing adjustment and inflation-adjusted profits are understated. Even if inflation had been constant, the allocation of financial adjustments between the MWCA and the gearing adjustment would have created a CCA average below that of CPP or RT as evidenced by the simulations in Table 6.2. During periods in which stock prices were displaying real rises (1973–6, 1979) CCA profitability falls dramatically below that of CPP and RT—CCA's entity concept of capital maintenance means that holding gains on stocks and fixed assets are not included in profit while the real capital which has to be maintained is based on specific price indices. At other times (1966–71) falling real stock and fixed asset prices result in lower depreciation charges under CCA and this, together with the exclusion of holding losses, raises CCA profitability above that of CPP or RT, outweighing the gearing adjustment understatement.

If we now simulate the effects of a constant 5 per cent inflation rate to 1972 followed by a constant 20 per cent inflation rate thereafter, and a zero inflation rate combined with actual relative price changes on the various profitability measures that would result from the actual accounts of our group of firms, we can confirm that the explanations for the differences between CCA, CPP, and RT suggested by the simple examples of the previous section hold good. Table 6.6 shows the profitability measures which would have resulted from the actual accounts of the 160 firms if inflation had been constant at 5 per cent p.a to 1972 and 20 per cent p.a. thereafter. With no changes in relative prices, CPP and RT profitability are identical. The first point to note is that even when inflation is constant, CCA rates of return are below their CPP/RT counterparts; this is a consequence of the inconsistent treatment of items in the MWCA and gearing adjustment mentioned above. More importantly, once

Table 6.6. Actual accounts, 5 per cent inflation to 1972,
20 per cent inflation from 1973

	HC (%)	CPP/RT (%)	CCA (%)
1966	7.3	2.7	2.4
1967	9.4	4.4	3.9
1968	11.5	5.8	5.6
1969	12.2	6.5	6.1
1970	12.5	6.6	6.2
1971	12.6	6.6	6.2
1972	15.6	8.7	7.9
1973	17.4	6.4	2.5
1974	15.0	2.4	−1.4
1975	14.3	−0.2	−3.2
1976	22.9	4.1	1.4
1977	20.6	1.8	−0.6
1978	19.9	0.8	−1.4
1979	18.5	−0.3	−2.3
1980	13.6	−4.1	−5.9
1981	13.4	−4.7	−6.6

inflation accelerates in 1973, the CPP/RT adjustment appropriately grows gradually, while CCA profitability drops suddenly from 7.9 per cent to 2.5 per cent between 1972 and 1973. The gearing adjustment thus makes CCA much too sensitive to changes in the rate of inflation and produces the tendency for CCA profitability to be below CPP and RT profitability that has been observed during the period of accelerating inflation.

Table 6.7 shows profitability measures for our group of firms on the assumption that there was no inflation over the period 1966–81 but the relative price movements of stocks and capital assets corresponded to the actual price changes over the period. As noted in the previous section CPP is unaffected by specific price changes so that CPP and HC rates of return are identical in this case. CCA and RT are both affected by relative price changes, but in different ways. Falling stock prices raised both CCA and RT profitability above CPP in the late 1960s and early 1970s, but by different amounts. The rapid increase in stock prices in 1973 led to a collapse in the CCA rate of return, but the RT rate of return increased above its 1972 value and was equal to the CPP figure. Rising stock prices also caused CCA profitability to fall below CPP profitability in 1976 and 1979, while RT profitability remained equal to CPP. Overall CCA can be seen to be highly sensitive to stock price movements, with the resulting rate of return being extremely volatile and often moving in the opposite direction to that of the appropriate measure, RT profitability. The failure of CPP to take account of

Table 6.7. Actual accounts, no inflation, actual relative price movements

	HC (%)	CPP (%)	CCA (%)	RT (%)
1966	7.3	7.3	8.5	7.7
1967	9.4	9.4	9.5	10.0
1968	11.5	11.5	13.1	12.2
1969	12.5	12.5	13.0	13.1
1970	12.5	12.5	14.3	13.1
1971	12.6	12.6	14.4	13.0
1972	15.6	15.6	14.2	15.9
1973	17.4	17.4	6.7	17.4
1974	15.0	15.0	12.6	14.7
1975	14.3	14.3	15.1	14.3
1976	22.9	22.9	19.3	22.9
1977	20.6	20.6	24.2	20.8
1978	19.9	19.9	21.1	20.2
1979	18.5	18.5	16.8	18.9
1980	13.6	13.6	16.0	14.6
1981	13.4	13.4	14.2	15.0

relative price changes results in there being some difference between the CPP and RT profitability measures, but these discrepancies are much less significant than those between CCA and RT.

6.4 Conclusion

The purpose of this chapter has been to provide a quantitative illustration of the nature and significance of the differences between HC, CPP, CCA, and RT profitability measures in order to supplement the theoretical arguments in favour of RT that were discussed in the previous chapter. We have seen that HC profitability figures are way in excess of the inflation-adjusted ones, emphasizing what is already well known, that HC accounts fail to record the real performance of companies. What is less well known, but emerges clearly from our analysis, is that despite the fact that inflation has abated substantially in recent years, the required inflation corrections to HC accounts remain important and will continue to do so for the rest of the 1980s, even if inflation falls to zero, as a consequence of the undervaluation of fixed assets and depreciation in HC statements.

The illustrations also show that, in quantitative terms, the most important difference between the three systems of inflation accounting is that between CPP and RT taken together and CCA. Although there are differences between CPP and RT as a result of CPP's use of historic costs rather than current values as its valuation base and its neglect of real holding gains and losses due to relative price changes these rarely produced a difference in average profitability across the 160 firms of more than one percentage point (although for some individual firms, of course, the differences were rather greater). The CCA profitability figures were, however, dramatically different from the CPP and RT ones in some years. One reason for this was the very curious properties of the CCA monetary corrections, with the gearing adjustment introducing a dependence of current corrections on the past history of the inflation rate, and the allocation of items between the MWCA and the gearing adjustment creating a discrepancy even once inflation had settled down to a constant level. Another was the use of a specific stock and fixed asset price index in CCA together with the exclusion of holding gains and losses on assets, which produced distorted profitability figures in certain years, particularly those when real commodity prices moved sharply. Evaluating CPP and CCA as methods of inflation accounting against the standard of RT, which we regard as the appropriate system, it is clear that CPP, although not ideal, is very much more useful than CCA in terms of the profit and profitability figures it produces. Although CCA balance sheet figures may have some value, the CCA profitability figures are at best crude approximations to an appropriate inflation-adjusted measure and at worst thoroughly misleading.

We have stressed throughout this chapter that the profitability measures which have been calculated are only to be regarded as illustrative. One reason for this is that they fail to deal adequately with the complications created by the appropriate treatment of deferred taxation in company accounts. It is to this issue that we turn in the next chapter.

Notes

1. An end-of-year error is introduced to the extent that nominal gains on stock holding from date of accumulation to accounting year end differ between opening and closing stocks. This will, in general, be small but can be avoided by including the net profit on stock holdings associated with revaluing to replacement cost at accounting year end.

2. Define DEP = Depreciation adjustment

E = Equity capital
K = Physical capital
M = Net monetary assets = NTC − D
NTC = Base of MWCA—essentially net trade credit extended
D = Net monetary liabilities not included in NTC
S = Stocks
Π = Rate of inflation

such that

$$S + NTC + K = D + E = E - (M - NTC) \qquad \text{(i)}$$

The total CCA adjustment is

$$DEP + \Pi(S + NTC) - ((DEP + \Pi(S + NTC))D)/(D + E)$$

where the last term is the gearing adjustment: from the identity (i) above this is equal to (for $D > 0$)

$$DEP + \Pi(S + M) - ((DEP - \Pi K)D)/(D + E).$$

The first three terms here are the depreciation, stock, and monetary adjustments respectively, while the last term is the inflation-rate-dependent distortion.

3. On an end-of-calendar-year basis (which is appropriate for most company accounts) the sharp rise in the cost of goods purchased by industry occurred in 1979.

4. This treatment of tax is another reason not to regard these profitability estimates as anything other than illustrative. The issues involved in recording tax appropriately in accounts are discussed in the next chapter.

7
Taxation and Accounting Profitability

7.1 Introduction

WE noted in Chapter 2 that one of the reasons why accounting profits differ from net cash flows is that accountants adjust the net cash flows in an attempt to show profit as it is earned rather than when net cash flows are generated. One such adjustment concerns 'timing differences' between accounting and taxable profits: some items are included in the accounts in a period different from that in which they are dealt with for taxation. The need to provide for deferred taxation in arriving at accounting profits is regarded by many accountants as an integral part of the matching principle, by which all known costs are matched against income in deriving net profits for any period of time. According to this view the tax charge recorded in the accounts should be based on the profit figure stated in the accounts rather than the profit figure which is assessed for taxation, and when these figures differ, as is the case, for example, when the allowable depreciation charge for tax purposes exceeds the related charge in the financial statement, the tax effects of these timing differences must be accounted for as deferred taxation.

The appropriate way of accounting for deferred taxation has been an issue second only to inflation accounting in the degree of controversy which it has generated in the UK over the past decade or so. The purpose of the present chapter is to discuss this issue in the light of the general principles which, we have argued, make accounting profitability data directly relevant for economic analysis. We begin by outlining alternative methods of incorporating taxation into measures of post-tax accounting profits, and explaining the basic issues in accounting for deferred taxation. A brief description of the various proposals for standard accounting practice concerning deferred taxation which have been made in the UK since 1973 is also given. Then we provide a theoretical analysis of the appropriate treatment of deferred taxation in accounting profitability measures which parallels our earlier discussion in Chapters 2, 3, and 4 of the conditions under which such measures are relevant for economic analysis. As perhaps would have been expected, if we have complete accounting profitability data, including tax charges, over the entire lifetime of an activity, then it is possible to calculate the post-tax internal rate of return from the post-tax accounting profitability data so long as the accounting treatment of taxation is such that there is a fully articulated relationship between the tax charge in the profit and loss account and the tax liabilities in the balance sheet. There is thus no reason to prefer one fully articulated method of treating taxation in the accounts to another if one wishes to use accounting profitability data to calculate an activity's post-tax internal rate of return over its lifetime. But in many cases this is not what one is interested in when using accounting profitability data: rather one is trying to judge the performance of an activity over a relatively short segment of its life, and in this case it is no longer possible to be indifferent between various fully articulated methods of treating taxation in the accounts. We argue that the appropriate method of accounting for deferred tax is one which follows naturally when our analysis in Chapter 4 is adapted to take account of taxation. Finally we provide an illustrative calculation of a post-tax accounting profitability measure along these lines for a sample of UK companies which, although subject to certain qualifications, is in principle more satisfactory than other estimates of the profitability of UK industry which have used accounting data.

7.2 Accounting for deferred taxation: an introductory outline

Both the objective of accounting for deferred taxation, which is to match the tax charge in a period to that period's accounting profit, and the differences between alternative methods of doing so can be clearly seen in the following simple example. Suppose that there is an investment project involving the purchase for £100 at the end of period 0 of an asset which generates a positive cash flow of £50 at the end of each of the next four periods. The tax system is such that all positive cash flows are immediately subject to tax, while the asset can be depreciated for tax purposes in equal amounts of £50 in periods 1 and 2. The tax rate is 50 per cent in periods 1 and 2 but rises to 60 per cent in periods 3 and 4. Accounting depreciation is computed on a straight-line basis over the four periods, with £25 being written off in each period.

The top panel of Table 7.1 shows that if only the tax payable in a particular period is charged against the project's pre-tax accounting profits then there is considerable fluctuation in the post-tax accounting profit figure, which is equal to pre-tax accounting profit in periods 1 and 2 but becomes negative in periods 3 and 4. This method of treating taxation in accounts, by which only the tax payable in a period is charged in that period, is known as the 'nil provision' or 'flow through' method, and clearly does not involve the setting up of any deferred tax account.

The aim of accounting for deferred taxation is to reflect the amount by which the tax liability in respect of a particular accounting period's profit has been affected by timing differences. Timing differences between accounting and taxable profits arise because some items are included in financial statements in a period different from that in which they are dealt with for taxation purposes. When a tax saving arises from an 'originating timing difference' it represents a credit which does not correspond with the pre-tax accounting profit figure. For example, when the tax system gives accelerated

Table 7.1. Accounting for deferred tax on an investment project

	Period			
	1	2	3	4
Tax rate	0.5	0.5	0.6	0.6
Net cash flow	50	50	50	50
Accounting depreciation	25	25	25	25
Accounting profit before tax	25	25	25	25
Tax depreciation	50	50	0	0
Taxable profit	0	0	50	50
Tax payable	0	0	30	30
Accounting profit after tax payable	25	25	−5	−5
Originating (+)/reversing (−) timing difference	25	25	−25	−25
Deferral method				
Transfer to or from deferred tax account	12.5	12.5	−12.5	−12.5
Deferred tax balance at start of period	0	12.5	25	12.5
Accounting profit after tax payable and transfer to or from deferred tax account	12.5	12.5	7.5	7.5
Liability method				
Transfer to or from deferred tax account	12.5	12.5	−10	−15
Deferred tax balance at start of period	0	12.5	25	15
Accounting profit after tax payable and transfer to or from deferred tax account	12.5	12.5	5	10

depreciation allowances, the depreciation allowance is not properly matched with an associated expense, as the accounting depreciation charge is smaller than the tax depreciation charge. This is the situation illustrated in the first two columns of Table 7.1: in each of periods 1 and 2 tax depreciation exceeds accounting depreciation by 25, leading to two originating timing differences of this amount. The object of accounting for deferred taxation is to relate the tax charge in the accounts to the pre-tax profit figure stated in the accounts. In order to do this the amount of the tax saving resulting from an originating timing difference should not appear as a benefit of the period in which it was granted, but rather should be carried forward and credited to the profit and loss account (in the form of a reduction in the tax charge) in periods when there are 'reversing timing differences' (for instance, if the accounting depreciation charge exceeds that for tax purposes, as in periods 3 and 4 of the example in Table 7.1). Thus the tax charge against pre-tax accounting profit in a particular period should comprise both the tax actually payable as a result of that period's tax computations and transfers to (when there are originating timing differences) or from (when there are reversing timing differences) a deferred taxation account. These deferred taxation account balances should be shown separately in the balance sheet and not included as part of shareholders' funds.

There are two methods of calculating the deferred tax balances. The deferral method involves the calculation of the tax effect of each timing difference by recording the deferred taxation applicable to originating timing differences at the tax rate then current, and its reversal at the same rate, irrespective of the rate of tax in force in the period of reversal. Hence in the example of Table 7.1 under the deferral method there is a transfer to the deferred tax account of 12.5 (equal to the originating timing difference times the tax rate of 50 per cent) in each of periods 1 and 2, and a transfer from the deferred tax account of the same amount in periods 3 and 4 (when there are reversing timing differences) despite the rise in the tax rate to 60 per cent in these periods. The alternative to this approach is the liability method, which, instead of deferring the taxation effects of current timing differences to the profit and loss accounts of future periods when the timing differences reverse, regards the taxation effects as liabilities for taxes payable in the future subject to adjustment if taxes change in the future. Thus the liability method maintains deferred tax balances as the sum in any one period of a series of timing differences multiplied by the current tax rate, which is regarded as the best estimate of future tax rates. Under the liability method, therefore, there are revisions to the deferred tax balances when the tax rate changes which have to be reflected in the profit and loss account. In the example of Table 7.1, use of the liability method requires a change to the deferred tax balance at the end of period 3 as a result of the rise in the tax rate to 60 per cent. The deferred tax balance at the end of period 3 is 15 (equal to the sum of timing differences to that point (25) times 60 per cent) and as a result the transfer from the deferred tax account in period 3 is only 10.

The example in Table 7.1 relates to a single project in which two originating timing differences in periods 1 and 2 are subsequently offset by two reversing timing differences in periods 3 and 4, and hence does not illustrate an important issue in accounting for deferred taxation. Suppose that the tax system grants accelerated depreciation allowances, and consider a firm with stable or growing investment over time. Such a firm will have a hard core of timing differences as originating timing differences on the firm's more recently acquired assets offset reversing timing differences on its older assets, with the result that some tax is permanently deferred. Since there is little likelihood of a payment of deferred tax arising in such circumstances there are many advocates of the partial provision basis, which accounts for deferred tax only to the extent that it is probable that any tax liability will be temporarily deferred by timing differences which will reverse in the future without being replaced. Under partial provision, therefore, deferred tax is accounted for only in so far as it will actually become payable, and it is calculated on the liability method, as this is consistent with the aim of providing only for the deferred tax which is likely to be payable. In contrast the full provision basis involves establishing each year a balance of deferred tax which will be sufficient to meet the reversal of all originating timing differences irrespective of whether there will be a net reversal. Full provision therefore typically involves a larger deferred tax balance, a smaller value of shareholders' capital, and a higher tax charge in the profit and loss account than partial provision.

The discussion so far has focused on accelerated depreciation for tax purposes as the sole source of timing differences, but there are in fact several possible sources. As well as accelerated depreciation allowances, timing differences may result when the tax system grants stock relief, for which there is no equivalent accounting charge; when there are revaluation surpluses on fixed assets for which a tax charge does not arise until the gain is realized on disposal; when there are taxable losses in one period which can be offset against taxable profits earned in other periods; and when there are short-term timing differences due to the use of a receipts and payments basis for tax purposes and an accruals basis in accounts, which usually reverse in the next accounting period.

In the UK the appropriate treatment of deferred taxation has been a contentious matter in the accountancy profession since 1973 when ED11 'Accounting for Deferred Taxation' was issued. This proposed that there should be full provision for deferred taxation on all material timing differences using the deferral method. It was followed by SSAP11 in 1975 which differed only by giving companies the choice of computing deferred tax using either the deferral or the liability method. There was however, considerable opposition to SSAP11, because balance sheets were regarded as becoming increasingly unrealistic, with provisions being made for deferred tax liabilities which would in many cases never be paid because subsequent originating timing differences would offset the reversal of current ones. In October 1976 the 1 January 1976 starting date was removed from SSAP11 while the ASC undertook a review of it. This led to ED19 in 1977 and SSAP15 in 1978, which required deferred tax to be provided (using the liability method) on all short-term timing differences and all other material timing differences unless it could be demonstrated with reasonable probability that the tax effects of timing differences would continue in the future. This switch to a partial provision basis for deferred taxation in the UK became effective for accounting periods beginning on or after 1 January 1979.

In 1983 a new exposure draft on the subject, ED33, was issued, but its purpose was only to revise SSAP15 rather than to make drastic alterations. Controversy over the appropriate treatment of deferred tax resurfaced following the 1984 Budget in the UK, in which there were major changes to the corporation tax system, involving a phased reduction in both the statutory rate of tax and the capital allowances granted by the tax system (in the case of plant and machinery these allowances were to be reduced from 100 per cent first-year allowances to 25 per cent annual writing down allowances). For many companies this tax reform created the difficulty of calculating future tax liabilities for which deferred tax provisions had not been made under SSAP15. The problem was particularly severe for the clearing banks, for the leasing activities which they had been using to shelter their profits from tax were likely to be significantly curtailed by the reduction in capital allowances. The questions of how much unprovided deferred tax to bring into the accounts, and how this should be presented, led to some criticism of the partial provision basis: more generally it revealed the lack of a clear set of principles on which the appropriate treatment of deferred tax could be based. However the revised SSAP15 which became effective from 1 April 1985 did not involve any substantial changes from the original one.

It is clear from the above discussion that the accounting profession in the UK is by no means agreed as to how deferred tax should be accounted for, and a striking feature of the deferred taxation debate in the UK is that although it has been taking place contemporaneously with the inflation accounting debate the latter debate appears to have exerted no influence on the former. In particular there has been no discussion of whether or how deferred tax balances should be maintained on a current value basis. In the following section we consider deferred taxation in terms of our theoretical discussion in Chapters 2, 3, and 4 in order to see how post-tax accounting profitability measures which will be relevant for economic analysis can be computed, and in so doing we hope to be able to throw some light on the question of what basis there might be for choosing between various alternative methods of accounting for deferred tax. We will return to the controversy following the 1984 corporation tax reform in the UK as an illustration of the issues involved.

7.3 Economically relevant post-tax accounting profitability

We begin by considering the relationship between the post-tax internal rate of return (IRR) and the post-tax accounting rate of profit (ARP) in the case where the available accounting data cover the entire lifetime of the investment. This case is exactly parallel to that discussed in Section 2.4 of Chapter 2, and, as in that section, to simplify the discussion and avoid the need to distinguish between *ex ante* and *ex post* assessment of the investment we assume that there is perfect certainty. In Section 2.4 of Chapter 2 it was shown that, under certain conditions, a number of general results linking the pre-tax IRR and the pre-tax ARP could be derived: in particular an investment's pre-tax IRR could always be obtained from a complete series of the pre-tax ARP and book value of capital employed over the investment's lifetime. It seems reasonable to expect that a similar general result linking the post-tax IRR and ARP should hold under similar conditions, and we shall now show that it does.

The post-tax IRR is defined as that constant one-period discount rate which makes the net present value of the after-tax net cash flows associated with an investment project equal to zero. Throughout this chapter we will use a circumflex over a variable to indicate that it is measured after tax. The post-tax ARP in the period ending at t, $\hat{a}_t$, is defined by

$$\hat{a}_t = \hat{Y}_t / (G_{t-1} - \mathrm{DT}_{t-1}) \tag{7.1}$$

where $\hat{Y}_t$ is post-tax accounting profit in period t, G_{t-1} is the aggregate book value of capital employed, gross of deferred taxes, at the end of period $t-1$ (i.e. at the start of period t), and DT_{t-1} is the deferred tax balance at the end of period $t-1$. The book value of shareholders' capital, V_t, is thus given by

$$V_t = G_t - \mathrm{DT}_t. \tag{7.2}$$

In Chapter 2 we noted that the relationship between the accountant's definition of profit in a period and the change in the book value of capital employed over the period was crucial in establishing general results linking the pre-tax ARP and IRR, and a similar relationship is crucial in the post-tax case. We assume that the following relationship between accounting profit after tax, net cash flow, tax charge, depreciation, overall book value of capital employed, and deferred tax balances always holds:

$$\hat{Y}_t = F_t - K_t - X_t - (\mathrm{DT}_t - \mathrm{DT}_{t-1}) + (G_t - G_{t-1}). \tag{7.3}$$

Here F_t denotes net revenue generated in period t, K_t new capital required in period t, and X_t tax payable in t. Equation 7.3 implies that the depreciation charge in t, D_t, must be such that all changes in the overall book value of capital employed flow through the profit and loss account:

$$D_t = K_t - (G_t - G_{t-1}) \tag{7.4}$$

and the total tax charge in the profit and loss account in period t, TC_t, must be such that any charge different from the amount of tax actually payable in that period must be fully reflected in the change in deferred tax balances over the period:

$$\mathrm{TC}_t = X_t + (\mathrm{DT}_t - \mathrm{DT}_{t-1}). \tag{7.5}$$

To see the implications of equations 7.3–7.5 it is helpful to consider in more detail the relationship in any period between the transfer to or from the deferred tax account, the change in the deferred tax balance, and pre-tax and post-tax accounting profits. Define X_t, the amount of tax payable in period t, as

$$X_t = \tau(F_t - A_t) \tag{7.6}$$

where τ is the tax rate and A_t is depreciation allowances available for tax purposes claimed in period t. Note that A_t denotes allowances actually *claimed* in period t: this means that if the allowances to which a firm is notionally entitled in a particular period exceed its taxable profits—in which case the firm is unable to claim all its allowances and must carry the unclaimed allowances forward until such time as it has sufficient gross profits against which to offset them—then A_t must be interpreted as only the allowances actually claimed in t. The unclaimed allowances are carried forward and, if they are offset for tax purposes in period $t+n$, become part of A_{t+n}. The transfer to or from the deferred tax account in period t is equal to $DT_t - DT_{t-1}$, and can be written as

$$DT_t - DT_{t-1} = \tau(A_t - D_t) \tag{7.7}$$

where D_t is accounting depreciation in period t as defined in equation 7.4. Substituting equations 7.6 and 7.7 into 7.5 we find that

$$TC_t = \tau(F_t - D_t) \tag{7.8}$$

so that the total tax charge in the profit and loss account is equal to the tax rate times pre-tax accounting profit, thus making clear the purpose of accounting for deferred tax as being to produce a tax charge which is directly related to pre-tax accounting profit. If equations 7.8 and 7.4 are substituted into 7.3 we see that

$$\hat{Y}_t = (1 - \tau)(F_t - D_t) \tag{7.9}$$

so that the relationship which we are requiring to hold in equation 7.3 simply means that post-tax accounting profit is equal to one minus the tax rate times pre-tax accounting profit, where the latter is defined in such a way that all changes in the aggregate book value of capital employed flow through the profit and loss account.

If equation 7.3 holds then the post-tax IRR of an investment project is equal to a weighted average of the post-tax ARPs in the individual periods of the investment's life, with the weights being the book value of shareholders' capital employed discounted at the post-tax IRR. This result means that the post-tax IRR can be found iteratively from the post-tax ARPs and book values of shareholders' capital (net of deferred taxes) over the lifetime of the investment project. The result can be derived very easily along the lines of Franks and Hodges (1983). Suppose that all cash flows occur at the end of accounting periods. The post-tax IRR of a project, $\hat{r}_t$, is defined by the equation

$$-K_0 - X_0 + \frac{F_1 - K_1 - X_1}{(1+\hat{r})} + \frac{F_2 - K_2 - X_2}{(1+\hat{r})^2} + \ldots + \frac{F_n - K_n - X_n}{(1+\hat{r})^n} = 0 \tag{7.10}$$

where it has been assumed that $F_0 = 0$. Substituting equations 7.1 and 7.3 into 7.10, noting that $G_n = DT_n = 0$ because the project is completed (i.e. generates its final cash flows) in period n, and rearranging gives

$$\sum_{t=1}^{n} \left[\frac{\hat{a}_t(G_{t-1} - DT_{t-1})}{(1+\hat{r})^t} - \frac{\hat{r}(G_{t-1} - DT_{t-1})}{(1+\hat{r})^t} \right] = 0$$

so that

$$\hat{r} = \frac{\displaystyle\sum_{t=1}^{n} \frac{\hat{a}_t(G_{t-1} - DT_{t-1})}{(1+\hat{r})^t}}{\displaystyle\sum_{t=1}^{n} \frac{(G_{t-1} - DT_{t-1})}{(1+\hat{r})^t}} . \tag{7.11}$$

Table 7.2 illustrates how the post-tax IRR can be calculated from suitably weighted ARPs and book values of shareholders' capital if the relationships in

Table 7.2. Example of calculation of an activity's post-tax IRR from post-tax accounting profitability data

	Period			
	0	1	2	3
New capital (K_t)	100	—	—	—
Net revenue (F_t)	—	48	63.2	69.12
Tax allowance claimed (A_t)	—	48	52	—
Tax paid $(\tau(F_t - A_t))$	—	0	5.6	34.56
Post-tax net cash flow	−100	48	57.6	34.56
$(F_t - K_t - \tau(F_t - A_t))$				
Accounting depreciation (D_t)	—	34	33	33
Originating ($+$)/reversing ($-$) timing	—	14	19	−33
difference $(A_t - D_t)$				
Transfer to deferred tax account	—	7	9.5	−16.5
$(\tau(A_t - D_t))$				
Tax charge $(\tau(F_t - A_t) + \tau(A_t - D_t))$	—	7	15.1	18.06
Pre-tax accounting profit	—	14	30.2	36.12
$(F_t - D_t)$				
Post-tax accounting profit	—	7	15.1	18.06
$(F_t - D_t - \tau(F_t - A_t) - \tau(A_t - D_t))$				
Aggregate book value of capital	—	100	66	33
employed at start of period (G_{t-1})				
Deferred tax balance at start of period	—	—	7	16.5
(DT_{t-1})				
Book value of shareholders' capital	—	100	59	16.5
employed at start of period (V_{t-1})				
Post-tax accounting rate of profit ($\hat{a}_t$)	—	0.07	0.2559	1.0945
$\hat{a}_t(G_{t-1} - DT_{t-1})/(1+\hat{r})^t$ ($\hat{r}=0.2$)	—	5.833	10.486	10.451
$(G_{t-1} - DT_{t-1})/(1+\hat{r})^t$ ($\hat{r}=0.2$)	—	83.333	40.972	9.5486

$$\sum_{t=1}^{3} \hat{a}_t(G_{t-1} - DT_{t-1})/(1+\hat{r})^t = 26.77; \quad \sum_{t=1}^{3} (G_{t-1} - DT_{t-1})/(1+\hat{r})^t = 133.85$$

$$26.77/133.85 = 0.2$$

equations 7.3–7.5 hold. The activity in this example involves an initial investment of 100 in period 0 and generates net revenues in the following three periods, after which the activity ends. The tax system is assumed to be one in which net revenues are subject to a 50 per cent tax rate, but depreciation allowances for tax purposes are such that the book value of the activity can be written off in two equal amounts in periods 1 and 2, subject to the limitation that allowances claimed in any period cannot exceed net revenue in that period. Hence in period 1 only 48 of the 50 tax depreciation allowance notionally available can be claimed, because net revenue in period 1 is only 48. The remaining 2 is carried forward and claimed in period 2. The post-tax net cash flows of the activity are shown in line 5 of Table 7.2 and are such that the activity's post-tax IRR is 20 per cent.

The accounting profitability figures for this activity are shown in detail in Table 7.2. The activity is depreciated on an (approximately) straight-line basis, so that there are transfers to the deferred tax account in periods 1 and 2 (when tax depreciation exceeds accounting depreciation) and a transfer from it in period 3 (when tax depreciation is less than accounting depreciation). Pre-tax accounting profit in each period is given by net revenue less accounting depreciation, while post-tax accounting profit in each period is given by subtracting a tax charge equal to the sum of tax payable in the period plus (minus) the transfer to (from) the deferred tax account from pre-tax accounting profit. The aggregate book value of capital employed at the beginning of each period is equal to the sum of capital expenditure less accounting depreciation charges up to and including the previous period. The deferred tax balance at the start of each period is given by the sum of transfers to or from the deferred tax account up to and including the previous period. Subtracting the deferred tax balance at the beginning of each period gives the book value of shareholders' capital at the start of the period. The post-tax ARP in any period is given by dividing post-tax accounting profit in that period by the book value of shareholders' capital employed at the beginning of the period. The calculations at the bottom of Table 7.2 show that the post-tax IRR is equal to a weighted average of the post-tax ARPs, with the weights equal to the book value of shareholders' capital discounted at the post-tax IRR, and hence that it is possible to obtain the post-tax IRR iteratively if data for the post-tax ARP and book value of shareholders' capital are available for the entire lifetime for an activity.

The example in Table 7.2 simply illustrates the general point that any method of deferred tax accounting which satisfies equations 7.3–7.5 will produce post-tax accounting profitability data over the lifetime of an activity from which it is possible to obtain the post-tax IRR. In the example there was no change in the tax rate during the activity's lifetime, so the difference between the deferral and the liability methods of accounting for deferred tax does not arise. However if equation 7.5 holds, both methods will permit the post-tax IRR to be obtained: so long as any revision to the size of the deferred tax balances as a result of a change in the tax rate under the liability method passes through the profit and loss account as part of the tax charge, then equation 7.11 applies. It is also the case that the flow-through method of treating taxation in accounts, in which no deferred tax account is created, will produce post-tax accounting profitability data from which the post-tax IRR can be derived. Under this method DT is identically zero in equations 7.3 and 7.5 and the post-tax ARP is measured as $\hat{Y}_t/G_{t-1}$. It is straightforward to check that the argument used above to obtain equation 7.11 continues to apply even when there is no deferred tax account, and also that in the example of Table 7.2 if post-tax accounting profit is measured as pre-tax accounting profit less tax paid in any period the resulting ARP and aggregate book value of capital figures when suitably discounted yield a figure of 0.2.

Thus we can see that, just as in the no-tax case considered in Chapter 2 when interest was focused on depreciation, if we have accounting data for the complete lifetime of an activity the way in which deferred tax is accounted for is essentially irrelevant for the purpose of deducing the post-tax IRR from post-tax accounting profitability figures so long as the basic relationships of equations 7.3–7.5 are satisfied. There may, of course, be reasons other than whether the post-tax IRR can be inferred from the accounting profitability data for preferring one method of accounting for deferred tax to another, but as far as this particular criterion is concerned there is no reason to prefer any one of the deferral, liability or flow-through methods to the other two.

7.4 Valuing deferred taxes over limited periods

The result that the way in which deferred tax is accounted for is essentially irrelevant if one wishes to obtain the post-tax IRR and accounting data for the complete lifetime of an activity are available is not one of great practical value. In many cases the available accounting data will cover only a short segment of an activity's lifetime, and in any case, as we argued in Chapter 3, it is not clear that the post-tax IRR, which is defined as a single number irrespective of the length of life of an activity, can be meaningfully used to evaluate the performance of an activity over a relatively short part of its total life. Evaluation of performance of continuing operations over short segments of their lifetime is, of course, a central purpose of accounting data; in Chapter 3 we argued that the appropriate way to consider the relevance of accounting profitability measures was to ask what economic interpretation could be given to the accounting rate of return (ARR) over a segment of the life of an activity which is computed from the net cash flows during that segment and the accounting values of the capital stock at the beginning and end of it. We showed in Chapter 4 that if the value-to-the-owner conventions were used to value initial and terminal capital stocks the resulting ARR would be directly relevant for economic analysis. We now wish to consider how this general conclusion is affected by the presence of taxation, and in so doing we argue for a particular treatment of deferred taxation as being the appropriate one.

The post-tax accounting rate of return over a segment of an activity's lifetime is defined as that discount rate which makes the discounted value of the net cash flows over the segment plus the discounted book value of shareholders' capital employed at the end of the segment equal to the book value of shareholders' capital employed at the beginning of the segment. In formal terms the post-tax ARR over the segment from period 1 to period T is given by $\hat{\alpha}$ such that

$$G_0 - DT_0 = \sum_{t=1}^{T} \frac{(F_t - K_t - X_t)}{(1+\hat{\alpha})^t} + \frac{G_T - DT_T}{(1+\hat{\alpha})^T} \tag{7.12}$$

where G_t, DT_t, F_t, K_t and X_t are as defined above, and all cash flows are assumed to occur at the end of the period. The post-tax ARR over a segment is defined in terms of initial and terminal book values of shareholders' capital and net cash flows, but it can be deduced from accounting data over the segment so long as post-tax accounting profits are related to after-tax net cash flows and changes in both the overall book value of capital employed and the deferred tax balance in the manner of equation 7.3. This can be seen by substituting equations 7.1 and 7.3 into 7.12 and rearranging to give

$$\hat{\alpha} = \frac{\sum_{t=1}^{T} \frac{\hat{a}_t(G_{t-1} - DT_{t-1})}{(1+\hat{\alpha})^t}}{\sum_{t=1}^{T} \frac{(G_{t-1} - DT_{t-1})}{(1+\hat{\alpha})^t}} \tag{7.13}$$

so that the post-tax ARR over a segment of an activity's lifetime can be calculated iteratively from the post-tax ARPs and the book value of shareholders' capital employed over the segment.

The computation of the post-tax ARR is illustrated by the numerical example in Table 7.3, which shows a three-period segment in the life of an activity. The book value of shareholders' capital employed at the beginning of this segment is 1 000 and the terminal book value of shareholders' capital is 1 014.8. The tax system in this example differs from that assumed in the previous illustrations in this chapter: it now involves a 50 per cent tax rate on net revenues received with an immediate 100 per cent allowance for capital expenditure, subject to the restriction that if allowances in any period exceed net revenues the excess must be carried forward and claimed in some future period. The post-tax ARR over this segment is 10 per cent, as can be checked from the after-tax net cash flows and initial and terminal book values of shareholders' capital:

$$-1\,000 + \frac{300 - 80 - 110}{1.1} + \frac{392 - 150 - 121}{(1.1)^2} + \frac{200 - 100 - 50 + 1014.8}{(1.1)^3} = 0$$

Table 7.3. Example of calculation of an activity's post-tax ARR from post-tax accounting profitability data over a segment of its lifetime

	Period		
	1	2	3
Net revenue (F_t)	300	392	200
New capital (K_t)	80	150	100
Tax allowance claimed (A_t)	80	150	100
Tax paid ($\tau(F_t - A_t)$)	110	121	50
Accounting depreciation ($D_t = K_t - (G_t - G_{t-1})$)	100	120	80.4
Transfer to deferred tax account ($\tau(A_t - D_t)$)	-10	15	9.8
Total tax charge ($\tau(F_t - D_t)$)	100	136	59.8
Pre-tax accounting profit ($F_t - D_t$)	200	272	119.6
Post-tax accounting profit ($(1-\tau)(F_t - D_t)$)	100	136	59.8
Aggregate book value of capital employed at start of period (G_{t-1})	2 000	1 980	2 010
Deferred tax balance at start of period (DT_{t-1})	1 000	990	1 005
Book value of shareholders' capital employed at start of period (V_{t-1})	1 000	990	1 005
Post-tax accounting rate of profit ($\hat{a}_t$)	0.1	0.1374	0.0595

$$\sum_{t=1}^{3} \hat{a}_t (G_{t-1} - DT_{t-1})/(1 + 0.1)^t = 248.234$$

$$\sum_{t=1}^{3} (G_{t-1} - DT_{t-1})/(1 + 0.1)^t = 2482.34$$

$$248.234/2482.34 = 0.1$$

and it can be deduced from the post-tax accounting data iteratively using equation 7.13, as is shown by the calculations at the bottom of Table 7.3, which confirm that a suitably weighted average of the individual post-tax ARPs will reveal the post-tax ARR to be 10 per cent.

What valuation conventions for the initial and terminal book value of shareholders' capital employed will enable the post-tax ARR to be given the significance attached to rates of return in economic theory? The discussion in Chapter 4 suggests that the appropriate conventions are the value-to-the-owner rules expressed on a post-tax basis, for it is clear that the analysis of Sections 4.2 and 4.4 of that chapter could be straightforwardly adapted to the case where taxes are involved by interpreting all variables on a post-tax basis. The value-to-the-owner rules on a post-tax basis can be expressed formally as:

$$V_t = \min\left\{\widehat{RC}_t, \widehat{EV}_t\right\} \text{ where } \widehat{EV}_t = \max\left\{\widehat{PV}_t, \widehat{NRV}_t\right\}. \quad (7.14)$$

Here V_t denotes the book value of shareholders' capital in t, $\widehat{RC}_t$ post-tax replacement cost in t, $\widehat{EV}_t$ post-tax economic value in t, $\widehat{PV}_t$ the present value in t (discounted at the after-tax cost of capital $\hat{\rho}$) of subsequent post-tax net cash flows, and $\widehat{NRV}_t$ post-tax net realizable value in t. Under the assumption that $\widehat{RC}_t \geqslant \widehat{NRV}_t$ for all t, the results of Chapter 4 all go through on a post-tax basis. Hence one can say, for instance, that if the *ex post* post-tax ARR calculated on the basis of the post-tax value-to-the-owner conventions is greater than the cost of capital (which in this case is the shareholders' after-tax discount rate) then either expectations were more than fulfilled during the segment over which the post-tax ARR was calculated, or post-tax present value at the start of the segment (based on expectations held at that time) exceeded post-tax replacement cost, providing prima-facie evidence of monopoly power.

The definitions of post-tax present value and post-tax net realizable value are straightforward. Post-tax present value is simply the discounted present value of all subsequent post-tax net cash flows associated with current assets, using the post-tax cost of capital as the discount rate. Post-tax net realizable value is simply the post-tax disposal value of current assets. Disposal of current assets may or may not involve a tax charge: in cases where assets have a tax written-down value of zero (because they have been fully depreciated for tax purposes) any receipt from their sale would attract a tax liability. The definition of post-tax replacement cost is a little more complicated. By replacement cost we mean the cost of acquiring assets which yield services equivalent to those used by the firm at their lowest current price. When the effects of taxation are considered it is necessary to take account of any allowances that the tax system grants on capital expenditures in defining post-tax replacement cost, such as annual writing-down allowances or initial allowances. These tax allowances mean that post-tax replacement cost is less than the cost of purchasing assets which yield equivalent services, but they will not be received until some time after the expenditure required to purchase the assets has been incurred, and hence these tax allowances must be discounted to reflect the cost involved in their receipt being delayed. Consistent with the definition of capitalization described in Chapter 3, the firm's tax liability is defined net of the present value of future allowances to which the acquisition of capital assets creates a legal claim. Post-tax replacement cost is therefore given by the current cost of acquiring assets which yield equivalent services to those currently used by the firm less the tax rate times the present value (discounted at the post-tax cost of capital) of the allowances granted by the tax system on the capital expenditure which would be required to purchase such assets. Note that post-tax replacement cost will depend on when in the future tax allowances can be claimed. This is particularly important when considering firms whose allowances exceed their taxable profits and so are subject to restrictions on the allowances that they can claim. The post-tax replacement cost of assets employed by such a tax-exhausted firm will be higher than that of identical assets employed by a firm which is not tax exhausted, because there will be a greater delay between incurring the expenditure required to purchase the assets and receiving the tax allowances for the former firm than for the latter.

This discussion of the conditions under which the post-tax ARR will be relevant for economic analysis has clear implications for the appropriate method of accounting for deferred taxation. If post-tax accounting profitability data are to provide appropriate signals about the performance of activities to investors and regulators then the deferred tax balance in any period must be such that when it is deducted from the overall book value of capital employed (determined on pre-tax value-to-the-owner conventions) the resulting book value of shareholders' capital employed is given by the value-to-the-owner rules on a post-tax basis. The total tax charge in the profit and loss account in any period is given by the sum of the tax payable and the transfer to or from the deferred tax account, where the latter is such that all changes in deferred tax balances from period to period are fully reflected in the transfer to or from the deferred tax account for that period. Thus we can add to our basic principles developed in Chapter 4 the following ones which relate to the treatment of taxation in the accounts: the deferred tax balance in any period must translate the book value of capital employed from value to the owner before tax to value to the owner after tax, and all changes in the deferred tax balance from period to period must flow through the profit and loss account via the transfer to or from the deferred tax account.

A consistent application of the value-to-the-owner rules on a post-tax basis involves the following procedure being followed. For assets valued at net realizable value any future tax liability incurred in the act of disposing of the assets, for example a balancing charge associated with a difference between net realizable and the tax depreciated value of the asset, should be recorded as a deferred tax liability in the balance sheet. For assets valued at replacement cost the expenditure incurred in replacing the firm's assets with ones that yield equivalent services will be diminished by the present value of the capital allowances that can be claimed on investing in these assets, as mentioned above. The deferred tax balance in this case should correspond to the present value of these allowances and hence show the reduction in the book value of the firm at replacement cost as a result of them. For assets valued at present value in their current operation the deferred tax balance is simply the present value of the expected future taxes associated with the net cash flows generated by the operation of these assets.

Broadly speaking the procedure employed when valuing assets at replacement cost can be described as a full tax provision, since the full discounted present value of allowances that can be claimed as a result of purchasing the assets is debited against replacement cost. Likewise the deferred tax recorded for assets valued at present value can be described as a full provision since no account is taken of returns accruing from future deferments of tax liabilities. Benefits accruing from the acquisition of assets at a future date will only be credited at the date that a legal claim is established. In any event the value-to-the-owner rules restrict the net valuation of an asset to be no greater than its post-tax replacement cost. It is the failure to ensure that this restriction is satisfied which has caused substantial errors and adjustments to have been made in the provision for deferred tax in the UK over the last decade.

It is helpful to illustrate how these conventions would apply in a simple example, which also demonstrates how substantial inaccuracies can result from other forms of deferred tax accounting. We take as our stylized example a bank which is engaging in the leasing of assets to other firms (i.e. is a lessor). We focus only on the leasing aspects of the bank's business, and consider the appropriate treatment of deferred tax around the time of the changes to the UK corporation tax system in 1984.

The example in Table 7.4 shows a case where the bank's leasing activities are in a steady state in the sense that new investment in leased assets is equal to depreciation on the existing stock. It is assumed that the value-to-the-owner rules result in leased assets being valued at replacement cost, which, given an assumption of no inflation, is equal to historic cost, and depreciation is assumed to take place on a straight line basis over four years. The leased assets are all assumed to be plant and machinery, and capital allowances have been computed on the basis of the provisions applying to this type of capital expenditure under the UK corporation tax system. Before 1984 100 per cent initial allowances were available on investment in plant and machinery. From 1984 the UK Government announced that initial allowances would be progressively phased out and investment allowances for plant and machinery would be restricted to annual writing down allowances computed on a declining balance basis. At the same time it was announced that the rate of corporation tax would be progressively reduced from 50 per cent to 35 per cent. The capital allowances and tax rates which have been assumed for the calculations in Table 7.4 are shown in the notes to the table.

The table shows that the effect of the tax changes is to reduce progressively the deferral provisions that the bank should make on a post-tax value-to-the-owner basis (assuming this involves replacement cost valuation). There are two reasons for this. The first is that the replacement of initial allowances by annual writing down allowances delays the date at which allowances can be claimed and hence reduces their present value. The second is that the rate at which allowances can be claimed is falling over the transition period thereby diminishing the value of the allowances. As a consequence of these two factors the balance sheet entry for deferred tax falls steadily, giving rise to a succession of negative entries under the overall tax charge in the profit and loss account.

Table 7.4. Illustration of a lessor's deferred tax provisions

			Deferred tax balance	
	Investment in leased assets	Book value of leased assets	(a) Value-to-owner rules	(b) SSAP15 partial provision
1983	100	250	125	0
1984	100	250	104	52
1985	100	250	94	47
1986	100	250	62	31

Transfers to/from deferred tax account

	(a) Value-to-owner rules	(b) SSAP15 partial provision
1983	0	0
1984	−21	52
1985	−10	−5
1986	−32	−16

Notes

(i) Capital allowances have been computed on the basis of the following allowances and tax rates:

Year	Initial allowance (%)	Annual writing down allowance (%)	Corporation tax rate (%)
1983	100	n.a.	50
1984	75	25	45
1985	50	25	40
1986 and thereafter	0	25	35

(ii) The value-to-the-owner rules value the assets at replacement cost.

(iii) In determining the partial provision of the deferred tax it is assumed that the lessor expected to be able to defer liabilities associated with previous capital allowances indefinitely until 1983. From 1984 onwards it is assumed that the lessor anticipates being able to defer 50 per cent of the liabilities associated with past expenditure.

(iv) The present value of writing down allowances has been computed on the basis of an assumed 10 per cent cost of capital throughout.

Let us contrast the treatment of deferred tax under the post-tax value-to-the-owner rules with the following caricature of the procedures that many lessors followed in the UK. Before the tax changes in 1984 many lessors expected that they would be able to defer the subsequent tax liability associated with 100 per cent initial allowances 'for the foreseeable future'. Under SSAP15 they were therefore encouraged to make little or no provision for deferred taxation, and this is reflected in a zero deferred tax balance in the example of Table 7.4. In 1984 many lessors were alerted to the fact that with the reduced capital allowances they might no longer be able to defer tax liabilities indefinitely. As a result 'prudent accounting practice' required them to make at least a partial provision, and for the sake of argument we assume that they were minded to make provision for 50 per cent of the full liability. The balance sheet entry for deferred tax for our lessor in Table 7.4 thus shows a substantial *rise* in 1984 thereby creating an addition to the tax charge in the profit and loss account. In view of the fact that capital allowances were more valuable before 1984 than thereafter and, if anything, leasing activity can be expected to decline as a result of these changes, at least in the long run, an increase in the deferral provision can only be regarded as a rather curious product of a very unsatisfactory set of guidelines.

7.5   Post-tax accounting profitability figures for a sample of UK firms

In Section 6.3 of the previous chapter we gave illustrative inflation-adjusted accounting profitability figures for a sample of 160 UK firms over the period 1966–81. The figures presented there were designed simply to show the quantitative significance of the differences between the various systems of inflation accounting, and for that reason were based on the reported tax figures in company accounts. As will be clear from the discussion in this chapter we do not think that the actual treatment of taxation in UK company accounts has been, or is, appropriate in terms of producing economically meaningful post-tax profitability figures. In this section we therefore present estimates of post-tax accounting profitability for the sample of 160 UK companies which not only make inflation corrections in the Real Terms manner that we advocated in Chapters 5 and 6, but also treat taxation in the way that we have argued to be appropriate in this chapter.

The estimates of post-tax accounting profitability which are given in this section are intended to illustrate the quantitative significance of changing the treatment of taxation from that recorded in company accounts in the UK over the period 1966–81 to the system which we have advocated in this chapter. The procedure that we have used is as follows. For each company the IFS Inflation Accounting Model was used to obtain an estimate of the replacement cost of the firm's capital stock (gross of tax) in each year at constant prices, in the manner described in Section 6.1 of the previous chapter. Apart from taxation the other components of the Real Terms accounts for each firm were estimated in precisely the same way as in Chapter 6. However, recorded deferred tax was eliminated from the balance sheet of each firm, and in its place was substituted a new deferred tax entry obtained by calculating in each year the present value of the tax allowances that a firm would be entitled to if it incurred the capital expenditure required to replace its capital assets and stocks in that year, expressed in constant prices.[1] The book value of shareholders' capital was then obtained by subtracting the new deferred tax balance from the gross of tax replacement cost of the firm's capital stock. Post-tax profits were adjusted by the difference between the addition to deferred tax recorded in company accounts in each year and that computed on a Real Terms basis (in this case replacement cost). Thus the post-tax real accounting rate of return on shareholders' capital for each year was measured as:

$$\frac{\prod_t^{RT} - (DT_t - DT_{t-1}) + (D_t^R - D_{t-1}^R)}{(G_{t-1} - DT_{t-1})} \qquad (7.15)$$

$$= \frac{F_t - D_t - X_t - (DT_t - DT_{t-1})}{(G_{t-1} - DT_{t-1})} \qquad (7.16)$$

where $\prod_t^{RT}$ is Real Terms profits in year t after recorded tax, as used in the column 'RT' in Table 6.5, D_t^R is the deferred tax balance in year t recorded in company accounts, DT_t is the deferred tax balance in year t obtained using value-to-the-owner rules and the other variables are as defined above. It is clear that the numerator of equation 7.16 corresponds to the definition of post-tax accounting profit in equation 7.3 (after substituting from equation 7.4) and the denominator corresponds to the post-tax measure of shareholders' capital at the end of the previous period. Equation 7.15 therefore represents the one-year post-tax ARP.

Table 7.5 records our estimates of Real Terms post-tax accounting profitability averaged across our sample of 160 firms (weighted by opening shareholders' capital and reserves). A number of considerations have to be borne in mind when interpreting these estimates. First, in valuing the deferred tax balance as the value of the capital allowances that can be claimed when incurring the expenditure required to replace a firm's assets, it is assumed that capital allowances can be realized in the year in which a claim arises. No account is therefore being taken of the effects of tax-exhaustion. As tax losses were widespread in the latter part of the 1970s and early 1980s (see the Green Paper on Corporation Tax, HMSO (1982)), measured profitability will tend to be understated in certain years.[2] Second, it is assumed throughout this section that an application of the value-to-the-owner rules leads to valuation on a replacement cost basis. In other words, Table 7.5 refers to the case of economic valuation being equal to or in excess of replacement cost for all firms in the sample. It is thus relevant to questions of investment, expansion, and entry, not those of disinvestment, exit, or retention of existing assets. A determination of how value-to-the-owner rules apply to a particular firm at a specific date requires more information than is available from company accounts.

Table 7.5 compares profitability estimates using the tax figures actually recorded in company accounts (as shown in Table 6.5 of the previous chapter) with those computed using post-tax value-to-the-owner principles. Rising interest rates at the end of the 1960s reduce the present value of writing down

Table 7.5. Post-tax accounting rates of return 1966–81

Year	RT with tax computed on value-to-owner principles	RT with tax computed on figures recorded in actual company accounts
1966	6.1	4.5
1967	5.4	7.0
1968	6.1	8.0
1969	12.6	8.5
1970	10.0	7.7
1971	2.3	6.6
1972	5.7	8.7
1973	−7.9	8.2
1974	3.4[a]	4.0
1975	2.1	−0.1
1976	9.4	6.3
1977	14.1	4.7
1978	9.0	5.9
1979	9.8	3.9
1980	3.0	0.1
1981	1.6[a]	1.3
AVERAGE	5.8	5.3

[a] The temporary implementation of a stock relief scheme in the UK between 1974 and 1980 creates a substantial timing effect in 1974 and 1981. This has been excluded from the above estimates.

allowances and raise the book value of shareholders' equity capital and profitability in relation to the figures obtained from unadjusted company accounts. At the beginning of the 1970s, investment incentives became steadily more generous, culminating in the introduction of 100 per cent first year allowances for investment in plant and machinery in 1972. The actual company accounts statements of shareholder capital are thus overstatements of tax-adjusted replacement cost measures, and this measurement error increases in size over the early years of the 1970s. Profitability computed on post-tax value-to-the-owner principles is therefore less than that obtained using stated tax liabilities. The lower profitability figures arising from the use of after-tax replacement cost measures of shareholders' capital are correctly indicating that the changes to investment incentives at the beginning of the 1970s encouraged deferment of capital expenditure to periods in which more generous allowances were available. Of course to the extent that the changes in investment allowances were unanticipated the *ex post* profitability estimates shown in Table 7.5 will differ from the *ex ante* ones and will not provide an accurate indication of the effect of changes in investment incentives on the timing of investment. The negative post-tax profitability estimate for 1973 using post-tax value-to-the-owner rules reflects the impact of the change in the statutory rate of corporation tax from 40 per cent to 52 per cent in this year: in combination with 100 per cent first year allowances this reduces the book value of shareholders' capital significantly and so leads to a large tax charge on profits via a transfer to the deferred tax account. Again this correctly indicates that if the tax change was anticipated then investment just before the change was very unprofitable by comparison with the alternative of deferring investment until after the tax change. After 1973 the value of tax allowances does not change appreciably but higher rates of return are recorded on lower valuations of shareholders' capital where full deferral provisions are made. In some years, tax adjustments result in quite small corrections to profitability but in others (for example 1977) the effects are appreciable. It is clear from the figures in Table 7.5 that evaluations of corporate performance can be sensitive to the rules that are used in accounting for deferred taxation.

7.6 Conclusion

The issue of how to provide for deferred tax in company accounts has been controversial over the past decade, and this chapter has attempted to show that the basic framework for the analysis of accounting profitability which was developed in earlier chapters of the book can provide clear guidance as to the appropriate treatment of deferred tax for the purposes of using post-tax accounting profitability figures in evaluating performance.

In Section 7.2 we explained the basic methods of accounting for deferred tax—the deferral and liability methods, and full and partial provision for such tax—and outlined the history of changes in official pronouncements on the approved form of accounting for deferred taxation in the UK over the 1970s. The major changes to the UK corporation tax system in 1984 highlighted the fact that the treatment of deferred tax in practice was not based on any clear set of principles. A particularly striking feature of the UK debate on deferred taxation was that although it was taking place at the same time as the debate on inflation accounting there was apparently no overlap between these two debates: in particular there was no discussion of whether deferred tax balances should be maintained on a current value basis.

In Section 7.3 of this chapter we applied the analysis of Chapter 2 to the case of an activity for which complete accounting profitability data were available over its entire lifetime, and showed that any method of accounting for deferred tax in which all changes in the deferred tax balance from period to period flow through the profit and loss account for that period will enable the activity's post-tax internal rate of return to be deduced from post-tax accounting profitability data. This might suggest that the question of the appropriate method of accounting for deferred tax is not one of any importance, but of course in most cases accounting data are being used to evaluate an activity's performance over a small part of its entire lifetime, and so the results from the complete lifetime analysis are of limited practical value. Section 7.4 of this chapter shows (following the lines of the analysis in Chapter 4) that if a post-tax accounting rate of return, defined in terms of initial and final book values of shareholders' capital (net of taxes) and intervening cash flows, is to be given the significance attached to rates of return in economic theory then initial and final book values of shareholders' capital must be measured in terms of the value-to-the-owner conventions on a post-tax basis. It follows from this that the deferred tax balance in any period is that amount which must be subtracted from the overall book value of capital (gross of taxes), which is found by applying the value-to-the-owner rules on a pre-tax basis, to give the book value of capital (net of taxes), which is obtained using the value-to-the-owner rules on a post-tax basis. This gives clear guidance as to how the deferred tax balance is to be computed on a current value basis: for assets with a book value of shareholders' capital given by post-tax replacement cost the deferred tax balance is given by the present value of the tax allowances that could be claimed if a company were to replace its assets by purchasing ones which yielded an equivalent service; for assets with a book value given by post-tax present value the deferred tax balance is the present value of expected future taxes associated with the net cash flows generated by the assets; and for assets with book value equal to post-tax net realizable value the deferred tax balance is given by the tax liability that would be involved in disposing of the assets.

If these principles are followed, and all changes in the deferred tax balances pass through the profit and loss account, post-tax accounting profitability figures can be given a meaningful economic interpretation. A simple example is given at the end of Section 7.4 to illustrate the difference between the treatment of deferred tax that was actually adopted by lessors in the UK following the 1984 corporation tax changes and the one which would be appropriate on the basis of post-tax value-to-the-owner conventions. In Section 7.5 we present estimates of post-tax Real Terms accounting profitability figures using post-tax value-to-the-owner rules for a sample of UK companies and contrast them with the corresponding figures obtained using the actual deferred tax entries in company accounts, which illustrate the qualitative significance of different treatments of deferred tax, and the importance of getting the treatment right if post-tax accounting profitability data are to be used for performance evaluation.

Notes

1. Statutory rates of initial and writing down allowances applicable in each year were used. The present value of writing down allowances was computed using the interest rate on 20 year government stock in the year of the investment as the discount rate.
2. For a description of how tax losses affect profitability measures see Mayer and Meadowcroft (1984).

8

Conclusion and Summary of Proposals

A LONG, complex, and at times acrimonious debate involving academics and practitioners in a range of disciplines has failed to resolve the question of the appropriate formulation of company accounts for measuring profitability, or indeed whether they should be formulated for this purpose at all. Such is the state of confusion that many have withdrawn from the debate claiming either that theoretical objections are irresolvable or that proposed solutions are impractical. The reluctance now of academics or regulators to employ accounting profitability data in economic analysis is a reflection of the former; the recent failure by the accounting profession in the UK to ratify widespread implementation of current cost accounting is an example of the latter. Instead, academics turn to other sources of information to evaluate performance, in particular market-based ones, and accountants return to former practices, hoping that previous problems will not re-emerge.

All of this is clearly very unsatisfactory and costly in terms of the quality of information provided and the purposes for which it is being applied. The object of this book has been to argue that the confusion and disillusionment are the result of a failure to specify sufficiently precisely the terms within which the debate is to be conducted. In particular a quite striking implication of this analysis is that much past discussion has failed to address the fundamental issue of the purpose for which accounts are being constructed.

To the extent that there has been any consideration of the objectives of accounting statements by economists it has usually been assumed that they are an attempt to approximate the Hicksian definition of profit. We argued in the introduction and elsewhere in the book that while the Hicksian concept is precisely appropriate for measurements of income, and possibly corporate distributions, it does not establish an appropriate basis for defining profit. Instead of wishing to be informed of what level of distributions can be maintained, the analyst of company performance is usually concerned about earnings in relation to what would have accrued in alternative activities.

Several examples of this have been provided throughout the text. The *ex ante* discussion considered questions of investment and disinvestment. The *ex post* sections referred to measurements of barriers to entry and exit and evidence of superior or inferior managerial performance. In each case performance is measured in relation to questions of the form what would have happened or will happen if the firm had done or does do something differently or if it did not have access to the resources which were actually at its disposal.

These counterfactuals or alternatives then define precisely the appropriate valuation bases for opening and closing stocks. As described at length they provide a persuasive justification for the application of replacement cost, present value, and net realizable value measurements of capital using the rules that are summarized below.

All of this is, of course, familiar and we are not arguing either that we have discovered a new measure of profit or that the accounting rules suggested are anything other than widely advocated. Instead, what the book has attempted to do is to marry the two and establish from basic principles the appropriate basis of accounting profitability measures. In the process, fortuitously or otherwise, we believe that a strong case has emerged for a particular set of accounting conventions. The conventions that have been suggested in the course of this book are summarized in the following section.

8.1 Summary of proposals

1. Value-to-the-owner rules should form the basis of the valuation of a company's assets and liabilities. These stipulate that if the replacement cost of the firm's assets exceeds their net realizable value on disposal then the assets of the firm should be valued at:

   (i) net realizable value if the value of the firm's assets in their current use falls short of their net realizable value on disposal

   (ii) replacement cost if their value in current use exceeds the cost of replacing the firm's assets with assets that generate an equivalent stream of services

   (iii) present value of future earnings if the value of the firm's assets in their current use lies between net realizable value and replacement cost.

2. Value-to-the-owner rules can be applied to any economically meaningful set of assets—a firm, subsidiary, plant, industry, or economy, or to a single investment. When undertaking an *ex ante* investment appraisal, the rules should be applied to the group of assets as a whole, i.e. value the group at one of replacement cost, present value, or net realizable value. This reflects the fact that purchase or, in the case of disinvestment, disposal of the group is being evaluated. In an *ex post* assessment of performance, replication of the firm may involve the employment of existing assets. The value-to-the-owner rules should therefore be applied to the individual asset and then summed. In practice, accounts are constructed on an *ex post* basis and the latter conventions are the ones that are relevant to published statements.

3. All changes in book values including those resulting from holding gains and losses (whether realized or unrealized) should have corresponding entries in the profit and loss statement. The statement could perfectly justifiably distinguish between realized and unrealized gains or between exceptional and normal losses and gains and valuable information might thereby be conveyed.

But profit and loss statements are only economically meaningful if they correspond to changes in book values.

4. These valuation principles continue to apply during periods of inflation. Profit figures calculated on the basis of value-to-the-owner rules will always provide appropriate nominal measures. Inflation-adjusted profits can then be derived by merely subtracting the rate of inflation of a *general* price index (i.e. the retail price index, consumer price index, or ideally an index reflecting the basket of goods consumed by shareholders) multiplied by the net worth of the firm from nominal profit. This is described as Real Terms accounting. No further inflation adjustment is required.

5. Deferred taxation should be provided for on the same value-to-the-owner basis. Thus if the relevant asset is valued at replacement cost then deferred taxation is equal to the allowances (first year and the present value of subsequent depreciation allowances) that could be claimed on replacing the asset with one that yielded an equivalent stream of services. If the asset is valued on a disposal basis then deferred taxation should be recorded as the balancing charge that is due (if any) on the immediate disposal of the asset. If the asset is valued at its current operating value (gross of future taxes) then deferred taxation is equal to the present value of future taxes associated with the return on the assets.

6. Assets and liabilities should be capitalized in the balance sheet if activities to the date in question give rise to a future legal claim by or on the firm. Thus, for example, a contingent liability is a legal claim which, although of uncertain future amount, does have an associated present value, replacement cost and current termination value. It should therefore be capitalized at one of these valuations. Likewise, research and development should not be capitalized at less than the economic valuation of the activities undertaken to date but at no more than the current cost of replicating these activities.

7. Goodwill is valued according to the same principles. Where the cost of reproducing a firm's reputation is high in relation to economic value then goodwill will be valued at economic value. Where advertising, guarantees, or production techniques can be used to establish an equivalent reputation at lower cost than the associated economic value, then inclusion at replacement cost is appropriate.

These proposals are shown in tabular form in Table 8.1.

8.2 Implications of proposals

If these proposals are implemented then accounts will provide information that is of value to investors, managers, regulators, and economists.

Accounts that are constructed on an *ex ante* basis (i.e. are forward looking and based on expectations) will convey the following signals:

Table 8.1. Summary of proposals

A. VALUATION BASIS

	Asset	*Tax Liability*
(i) Present value net of taxes > replacement cost less investment allowances	Replacement cost	First year allowances plus present value of future depreciation allowances
(ii) Present value net of taxes < net realizable value net of balancing charge on disposal	Net realizable value	Balancing charge on disposal
(iii) Present value net of taxes between replacement cost and net realizable value	Present value of future earnings	Present value of future taxes

B. PROFIT AND LOSS STATEMENT

Nominal profit = Change in assets less change in liabilities
Real profit = Nominal profit less rate of inflation times net worth

C. ACCOUNTING RATE OF PROFIT

$$\text{The accounting rate of profit} = \frac{\text{Real profit}}{\text{Net worth}}$$

(i) an accounting rate of profit in excess of the cost of capital implies that new investment is profitable;

(ii) an accounting rate of profit equal to the cost of capital implies that the starting of a new activity is not profitable but existing activities should be continued;

(iii) if valuations are made on net realizable value basis then an accounting rate of profit less than the cost of capital implies that an existing activity should be curtailed.

Accounts that are constructed on an *ex post* basis (i.e. using actual out-turn data) convey the following signals, provided that expectations were fulfilled over the period in question:

(i) an accounting rate of profit in excess of the cost of capital is prima-facie evidence of a barrier to entry at the beginning of the period;

(ii) an accounting rate of profit less than the cost of capital is prima-facie evidence of a barrier to exit at the beginning of the period, provided that the closing assets are valued at economic value.

Persistence of abnormally high or low rates of return suggests barriers to entry or exit rather than unfulfilled expectations. Further indications of whether expectations were fulfilled may be available from valuations at market prices. Exceptional performance can be attributed to managerial skills if abnormal returns still persist when valuations are made on the basis of opportunities available to competitors. Furthermore, the principles of capitalization described above permit performance to be associated with activities undertaken in the relevant period. Thus legal claims created by past activities will already have been capitalized and included in a previous period's performance. On the other hand, in contrast to market valuations, anticipated but as yet unrealized claims will not be recorded until they are established.

We have noted that estimates of rates of profit are sensitive to the conventions that are employed. In particular we observed that the application of inappropriate price indices in inflation adjustments or valuations on bases other than the value-to-the-owner rules could result in seriously misleading rates of profit estimates. Neither of the two commonly advocated accounting systems, Current Cost accounting (CCA) and Constant Purchasing Power (CPP), accurately reflect rates of profit derived from value-to-the-owner and Real Terms accounting. CPP does not apply the value-to-the-owner rules consistently (at least not as it is commonly interpreted) and CCA uses inappropriate price indices and fails to ensure that all balance sheet changes are passed through the profit and loss statement. As implemented in the UK, CCA is also seriously distorted by the gearing adjustment which gives it a spurious dependence on past as well as current inflation rates. The importance of the correct application of Real Terms accounting is not merely restricted to periods of high inflation.

We saw that balance sheet valuations were sensitive to the manner in which deferred taxation was computed. For example, a lessor should not record the net value of a leased asset as being greater than the replacement cost of the asset less the capital allowances (first year and present value of depreciation allowances) associated with replacement. In other words the net value cannot be greater than that resulting from a full provision for deferred taxation on a replacement cost basis. If this convention had been followed in the late 1970s and early 1980s the major lessors would have recorded a very much lower net worth and would not have been required to make substantial deferred tax adjustments in 1984 when there was a fundamental revision to corporation tax in the UK.

References

Accounting Standards Committee (1977). *ED19 Accounting for Deferred Taxation*. London: ASC.
—— (1978). *Statement of Standard Accounting Practice No. 15, Accounting for Deferred Taxation (SSAP15)*. London: ASC.
—— (1980). *Statement of Standard Accounting Practice No. 16, Current Cost Accounting (SSAP16)*. London: ASC.
—— (1983). *ED33 Accounting for Deferred Tax*. London: ASC.
—— (1984). *ED35 Accounting for the Effects of Changing Prices*. London: ASC.
Accounting Standards Steering Committee (1973). *ED11 Accounting for Deferred Taxation*. London: ASSC.
—— (1975). *Statement of Standard Accounting Practice No. 11, Accounting for Deferred Taxation (SSAP11)*. London: ASSC.
Baxter, W. T. (1967). 'Accounting values: sale price versus replacement cost', *Journal of Accounting Research* **5**, 208–14.
—— (1971). *Depreciation*. London: Sweet and Maxwell.
—— (1975). *Accounting Values and Inflation*. New York: McGraw-Hill.
Beaver, W. (1981). *Financial Reporting: An Accounting Revolution*. Englewood Cliffs: Prentice-Hall.
Bonbright, J. C. (1937). *Valuation of Property* (2 volumes). New York: McGraw-Hill.
Brealey, R. A., and Myers, S. C. (1981). *Principles of Corporate Finance*. New York: McGraw-Hill.
Bromwich, M. (1977). 'The use of present value valuation models in published accounting reports', *The Accounting Review* **52**, 587–96.
Canadian Institute of Chartered Accountants (1979). *Exposure Draft: Current Cost Accounting*.
—— (1982). *Reporting the Effects of Changing Prices*.
Canning, J. B. (1929). *The Economics of Accountancy: A Critical Analysis of Accounting Theory*. New York: Ronald Press.
CCAB (1975). *Initial Reactions to the Report of the Inflation Accounting Committee*. London: Accounting Standards Committee.
Chambers, R. J. (1966). *Accounting, Evaluation and Economic Behaviour*. Englewood Cliffs: Prentice-Hall.
Committee of Inquiry into Inflation and Taxation (1975). *Report: Inflation and Taxation* (The Mathews Report). Canberra: Australian Government Publishing Service.
ED11, see Accounting Standards Steering Committee (1973).
ED19, see Accounting Standards Committee (1977).
ED33, see Accounting Standards Committee (1983).
ED35, see Accounting Standards Committee (1984).
Edey, H. C. (1974). 'Deprival value and financial accounting' in H. C. Edey and B. S. Yamey (eds.), *Debits, Credits, Finance and Profits*. London: Sweet and Maxwell.

Edwards, E. O., and Bell, P. W. (1961). *The Theory and Measurement of Business Income*. University of California Press.
—— and Johnson, L. T. (1979). *Accounting for Economic Events*. Houston: Scholars Book Co.
Fairburn, J. (1985). 'Statutory monopolies and market power', unpublished paper, Institute for Fiscal Studies.
Fama, E. F. (1970). Efficient capital markets: a review of theory and empirical work', *Journal of Finance* **25**, 383–417.
—— (1972). 'Components of investment performance', *Journal of Finance* **27**, 557–68.
—— and Miller, M. H. (1972). *The Theory of Finance*. New York: Holt, Rinehart and Winston.
FASB (1978). *Proposed Statement of Financial Accounting Standards: Financial Reporting and Changing Prices*. Stamford: Financial Accounting Standards Board.
—— (1979). *Statement of Financial Accounting Standards No. 33 (FAS33): Financial Reporting and Changing Prices*. Stamford: Financial Accounting Standards Board.
Feldstein, M. S., and Summers, L. H. (1977). 'Is the rate of profit falling?', *Brookings Papers on Economic Activity*, No. 1, 211–28.
Fisher, F. M., and McGowan, J. J. (1983). 'On the misuse of accounting rates of return to infer monopoly profits', *American Economic Review* **73**, 82–97.
Flemming, J. S., and Wright, J. F. (1971). 'Uniqueness of the internal rate of return: a generalisation', *Economic Journal* **81**, 256–63.
Flemming, J. S., Price, L. D. D., and Ingram, D. H. A. (1976). 'Trends in company profitability', *Bank of England Quarterly Bulletin* **16**, 36–52.
Franks, J. R., and Hodges, S. D. (1983). 'The meaning of accounting numbers in target setting and performance measurement: implications for managers and regulators', unpublished paper, London Business School.
Gee, K. and Peasnell, K. V. (1976). 'A pragmatic defence of replacement cost', *Accounting and Business Research* **6**, 242–9.
Gibbs, M. (1976). 'A better answer to the problem of inflation accounting', *The Times*, 23 February 1976.
Gibbs, M., and Seward, W. (1979). *ED24—Morpeth's New Proposals*. London: Phillips and Drew.
Godley, W., and Cripps, T. F. (1975). 'Profits, stock appreciation and the Sandilands report', *The Times*, 1 October 1975.
Grossman, S. J., and Stiglitz, J. E. (1980). 'On the impossibility of informationally efficient markets', *American Economic Review* **70**, 393–408.
Harcourt, G. C. (1965). 'The accountant in a golden age', *Oxford Economic Papers* **17**, 66–80.
Hay, D. A., and Morris, D. J. (1979). *Industrial Economics: Theory and Evidence*. Oxford: Oxford University Press.
Hicks, J. R. (1946). *Value and Capital*. Oxford: Clarendon Press.
Hill, T. P. (1979). *Profits and Rates of Return*. Paris: Organisation for Economic Co-operation and Development.
Hirshleifer, J. (1958). 'On the theory of optimal investment decision', *Journal of Political Economy* **56**, 329–52.
HMSO (1982). *Corporation Tax*. Cmnd 8456. London: Her Majesty's Stationery Office.
Holland, D. M., and Myers, S. C. (1979). 'Trends in corporate profitability and capital

costs' in R. Lindsay (ed), *The Nation's Capital Needs: Three Studies.* New York: Committee for Economic Development.

Hotelling, H. (1925). 'A general mathematical theory of depreciation', *Journal of the American Statistical Association* **20,** 340–53.

Institute of Chartered Accountants in Australia and Australian Society of Accountants (1976). *Provisional Accounting Standard: Current Cost Accounting.*

—— (1983). *Statement of Accounting Practice No. 1 (SAP1).*

Kay, J. A. (1976). 'Accountants, too, could be happy in a golden age', *Oxford Economic Papers* **17,** 66–80.

—— (1977). 'Inflation accounting—a review article', *Economic Journal* **87,** 300–11.

—— and Mayer, C. P. (1986). 'On the application of accounting rates of return', *Economic Journal* **96,** 199–207.

Kennedy, C. (1978). 'Inflation accounting: retrospect and prospect', *Cambridge Economic Policy Review* **4,** 58–64.

Lindenberg, E., and Ross, S. (1981). 'Tobin's q ratio and industrial organisation', *Journal of Business* **54,** 1–32.

Livingstone, J. R., and Salamon, G. L. (1970). 'Relationship between the accounting and the internal rate of return measure: a synthesis and an analysis', *Journal of Accounting Research* **8,** 199–216.

Mayer, C. P. (1982). 'A program for inflation adjusting published accounts', *Institute for Fiscal Studies Working Paper No. 31.*

—— and Meadowcroft, S. (1984). 'Equity rates of return in the U.K.—evidence from panel data', *Recherches Economiques de Louvain* **50,** 363–98; and in D. Weiserbs (ed.), *Industrial Investment in Europe: Economic Theory and Measurement*, Martinus Nijhoff, 1985.

Meadowcroft, S. (1983). 'A program for inflation adjusting published company accounts: an interim report', unpublished paper, Institute for Fiscal Studies.

New Zealand Society of Accountants (1981). *Exposure Draft: Current Cost Accounting.*

—— (1982). *Current Cost Accounting Standard No. 1: Information Reflecting the Effects of Changing Prices.*

Parker, R. H., and Harcourt, G. C. (1969). *Readings in the Concept and Measurement of Income.* Cambridge: Cambridge University Press.

Peasnell, K. V. (1977). 'A note on the discounted present value concept', *The Accounting Review* **52,** 186–9.

—— (1982). 'Some formal connections between economic values and yields and accounting numbers', *Journal of Business Finance and Accounting* **9,** 361–81.

Richardson Committee Report (1976). *The Report of the Committee of Inquiry into Inflation Accounting.* Wellington: New Zealand Government Printer.

Salinger, M. A. (1984). 'Tobin's q, unionization, and the concentration-profits relationship', *The Rand Journal of Economics* **15,** 159–70.

Sandilands Committee (1975). *Inflation Accounting: Report of the Inflation Accounting Committee under the Chairmanship of F. E. P. Sandilands.* London: HMSO (Cmnd 6225).

Scott, M. F. G. (1976). *Some Economic Principles of Accounting: a Constructive Critique of the Sandilands Report.* London: Institute for Fiscal Studies (IFS Lecture Series No. 7).

SEC (1976). *Accounting Series Release No. 190 (ASR190), Amendments to Regulations S-X Requiring Certain Replacement Cost Data.* Washington: SEC.

Smirlock, M., Gilligan, T., and Marshall, W. (1984). 'Tobin's q and the structure-performance relationship', *American Economic Review* **74**, 1051–60.

Solomon, E. (1966). 'Return on investment: the relation of book yields to true value' in R. K. Jaedicke, Y. Ijiri, and O. Nielsen (eds.), *Research in Accounting Measurement*, American Accounting Association.

—— (1970). 'Alternative rate of return concepts and their implications for utility regulation', *Bell Journal of Economics and Management Science* **1**, 65–81.

Solomons, D. (1966). 'Economic and accounting concepts of cost and value' in M. Backer (ed.), *Modern Accounting Theory*. Englewood Cliffs, Prentice-Hall.

SSAP11, see Accounting Standards Steering Committee (1975).

SSAP15, see Accounting Standards Committee (1978).

SSAP16, see Accounting Standards Committee (1980).

Stamp, E. (1971). 'Income and value determination and changing price levels: an essay towards a theory', *The Accountant's Magazine*, 277–92.

Stauffer, T. R. (1971). 'The measurement of corporate rates of return: a generalised formulation', *Bell Journal of Economics and Management Science* **2**, 434–69.

Sweeney, H. W. (1936). *Stabilized Accounting*. New York: Harper.

Treynor, J. L. (1972). 'The trouble with earnings', *Financial Analysts' Journal* **28**, 41–3.

Turvey, R. (1971). *Economic Analysis and Public Enterprise*. London: George Allen and Unwin.

Tweedie, D., and Whittington, G. (1984). *The Debate on Inflation Accounting*. Cambridge: Cambridge University Press.

Whittington, G. (1983). *Inflation Accounting: An Introduction to the Debate*. Cambridge: Cambridge University Press.

Williams, N. P. (1981). 'Influences on the profitability of twenty-two industrial sectors', Bank of England Discussion Paper No. 5.

Wright, F. K. (1964). 'Towards a general theory of depreciation', *Journal of Accounting Research* **2**, 80–90.

—— (1970). 'A theory of financial accounting', *Journal of Business Finance* **2**, 57–69.

—— (1978). 'Accounting rate of profit and internal rate of return', *Oxford Economic Papers* **30**, 464–8.

Index